LOSE THE CAPE!

Volume 4

2nd Edition

LOSE THE CAPE!

The Mom's Guide to Becoming Socially & Politically Engaged (& How to Raise Tiny Activists)

2ND EDITION

edited by:

ALEXA BIGWARFE

&

NANCY CAVILLONES

Copyright © 2020 Alexa Bigwarfe

No part of this publication may be reproduced, distributed, or transmitted in any form or by any means, including photocopying, recording, or other electronic or mechanical methods, without the prior written permission of the publisher, except in the case of brief quotations embodied in critical reviews and certain other noncommercial uses permitted by copyright law.

The fact that an organization or website is referred to in this work as citation or a potential source of further information does not mean that the Author of Publisher endorses the recommendations that it may make.

This is the 4th Book in the Lose the Cape! series. Learn more about all books on http://losethecape.com

Cover Art: Adrienne Hedger
Interior Design: Write.Publish.Sell www.writepublishsell.co
Editing: Alexa Bigwarfe & Nancy Cavillones

Published by Kat Biggie Press
Columbia, SC
info@katbiggiepress.com
http://katbiggiepress.com

ISBN 13: 978-1-948604-40-6
Library of Congress Control Number: on file
Second Edition: June 2020

Printed in the United States

DEDICATION

To all the Moms out there making the world a better place for their children. In 2020, we especially salute the mothers of color.

CONTENTS

Foreword: S. Nadia Hussain

Introduction ... 1

PART I: A CALL TO ADVOCACY/ACTIVISM

Use Your Voice and Get Involved
Alexa Bigwarfe ... 11

We've Got to Hold the Line
Bellamy Shoffner ... 17

If We Don't Do It, Who Will?
Heather Vickery ... 21

Tikkun Olam
Nancy Cavillones ... 33

Accidental Activist
Mason Aid ... 39

Showing Up So My Daughter Can Recognize her Purpose and Resilience in Making an Impact In This World
Desiree Peterkin-Bell ... 45

Bring Your Own Chair to the Table
Chou Hallegra ... 51

Learning to Emerge
Elizabeth Schroeder ... 57

PART II: HOW DO YOU GET INVOLVED?

Political Engagement - We Need You
Jennifer Rosen Heinz ... 65

From Frustrated-as-Hell to Getting-Shit-Done: One Mom's Advice on Choosing Your Cause and Becoming an Activist

Shanti Brien ... 79

Be The Voice
Chou Hallegra ... 85

The Wizard of Oz: Dorothy as a Social Activist
Mary Wheatley ... 91

PART III: RAISING TINY ACTIVISTS

Raising Warriors: How Parents Everywhere Can Save the World One Child at a Time
Katie White ... 97

Kindness and Generosity
Maria Dismondy... 107

The Power of In-Between Time
Sarah O'Dell ... 113

The Examples We Set
Yvonne Marcus ... 119

Take Your Children With You
Alexa Bigwarfe ... 125

Teach Your Children Well: How Raising Activists Can Not Only Make the World Better, It Can Improve Children's Lives
Gretchen Kelly ... 131

Teaching Your Children About Inequality Around Gender, Race, and Culture
Laura Lyles Reagan ... 143

Conclusion ... 149

About the Editors ... 155

Acknowledgments ... 157

Resources ... 161

"A COUNTRY'S GREATNESS LIES IN ITS UNDYING IDEALS OF LOVE AND SACRIFICE THAT INSPIRE THE MOTHERS OF THE RACE."

— SAROJINI NAIDU

FOREWORD
S. NADIA HUSSAIN

In my current work and commitments, I am often asked, "When did you realize you wanted to be socially and politically engaged" or "what inspired your engagement?". This answer came to me very young, as something ingrained in me by my parents, and by the legacies of my ancestors, who took part in protests against colonialism in the early 20th century and boycotted British goods as part of Gandhi's political movement for India's eventual independence. From an early age, my parents, Muslim immigrants from Bangladesh, imparted upon me the importance of kindness to others. The need to be of service and to help those in difficult circumstances, especially folks facing poverty and hardship. My mother would tell me how I lucky I was to be in the United States, to have opportunities for education, food and shelter, something that wasn't a given back in her homeland. Her words always stuck with me like a mantra, that one should always contribute to something greater than oneself.

The inspirational legacy of my family and the words of my parents, though powerful, weren't the only things that inspired me to do the work I do today. The struggles that my family and

I experienced in this country galvanized my engagement, as I repeatedly witnessed the American dream my parents worked so hard for, come crashing down.

Before my parents immigrated to the United States, my father was a doctor in Bangladesh and my mother, who had already gotten a double masters in child and developmental psychology, was getting started on her PHd. They left all of this, like so many immigrants, to embark on a journey to a new home, worlds away, where they believed they would have better opportunities and more importantly, the best education possible for their future children.

They came with high hopes, but the reality of life in the United States for new immigrants quickly proved to be much harder than they expected. Like many new immigrants, my father worked odd jobs, a foreign medical degree not being of much value in the U.S.. He essentially had to start over, all while being a new father in a country, struggling with a new language and culture. He ended up joining the U.S. Army and serving abroad with my mom and me in tow, so that he could expedite his citizenship while providing for us. He studied non-stop to become a doctor for the second time. All the while, unbeknownst to us, he was struggling with severe mental illness. While he worked to pay the bills, the monster of bipolar disorder was never addressed as we went about our lives accepting his outbursts and odd behavior as somehow normal.

While my father served in the military, my family, now with the addition of my younger sister, relied on food stamps and social safety nets to help make ends meet. I have distinct memories of waiting in line with my father for food stamps at the social services office. I am grateful that we had access to these supports when we needed help. It helped us stay on our feet as my father served this nation and worked hard on his journey to achieve his American dream of being a successful doctor in the United States.

And we almost made it.

My father did finally pass his exams to be re-certified as a medical doctor. He began residencies, 3-year stints at hospitals where doctors get their training they need to complete before being able to practice medicine. Yet, as hard as he tried, he was unable to complete them due to his worsening mental illness. Over and over, his contract wasn't renewed, causing my family to move almost every year in search of another residency. During this time, we would go back onto food stamps and live in government housing projects.

While this was happening, my mother worked retail and restaurant jobs to help provide some money to our household. Raising two girls with a mentally ill husband didn't leave her much time to pursue her graduate degrees in this country. The two masters she already had meant nothing in the United States. To work in psychology or social work again meant she would have to start from scratch. It broke my heart to see my educated mother hopefully beginning community college classes, only to have to stop to help support her children and my father.

When she finally got a job as a mobile therapist, working with kids and families in crisis in our small town in Pennsylvania, the ugly reality of discrimination and racism came to a head as employers and clients complained that they didn't "understand her accent", as she was passed over for promotions by people with less experience and education than her. Families in the area couldn't take the idea that a brown woman with a different sounding name was telling them how to raise their children. My mom was so proud of her job, she cared so much about the kids, and they cared for her, yet she would be let go or fired from work. She didn't know her rights, and even if she did, we didn't have the means, access, or money to afford a lawyer who could bring forth a case.

After she lost her dream career, she went back to doing labor-intensive work, work that was so intense that it cost her permanent injuries in her hands, causing her to go into early retirement and rely on disability benefits. She still has trouble closing her hands into fists due to this. Any attempt she made to get workers compensation went nowhere. We didn't have the money, and we didn't have knowledge of the system to fight. We were alone.

Our struggles came to an apex in the summer of 2005 when my father was arrested for allegations of Medicaid fraud. The fragile world my parents so painstakingly built imploded. My mentally ill father was treated as a criminal by the state, when instead, he should have been in a hospital. There were no victims, no one was hurt, and like so many swept up by mass incarceration, he pled guilty to avoid going to trial, fearful that a small majority-white town in the middle of Pennsylvania in the throes of post 9/11 anti-Muslim hysteria would never him a chance to prove his innocence. During his case, our entire family, all US Citizens, including my sister and I, who were born here, were forced to surrender our passports, something

I strongly doubt would happen if we were a white American family.

Even worse, the jails and prisons he stayed at wouldn't give him his proper mental health medication, essentially torturing him with their lack of medical care, something all too common within our penal system. One year into his three year sentence, he was beaten so badly by prison guards that they broke his arm and fractured his skull, causing his brain to hemorrhage and requiring emergency brain surgery. The prison alleged that he fell in the shower and denied everything. There was no hope for restitution or justice. Once in the system, I learned, human rights no longer exist, and what happens behind closed doors often stay there in darkness.

Everything I detailed about what happened to my family and I occurred before the 2016 election cycle. Since then, what I have seen, as an activist, mother and daughter, are already-broken systems left to worsen as human and civil rights take a backseat to fear, division and scapegoating. I see the echoes of what my family experienced all around me whenever I read the news or mobilize around a crisis. I see story after story of undocumented immigrants suffering and dying in cages as medical care is denied to them and their children. I see laws that protected vulnerable communities from things like job discrimination being thrown out. I see repeated attacks to cut social safety nets that helped my family and I, and so many families around the country, survive.

Every person does not have to experience my story or the struggles of others to feel empowered to make a difference. The truth is, we all have tough experiences in our lives, tragedies we have faced, pain and hardship that may have tested us. One doesn't have to go through the worst to want to create change. Caring matters, empathy matters, wanting to see a different, positive and beautiful outcome for all our families and communities matter.

If we ourselves are not the driving force behind the changes that we must see, then nothing will ever improve, no one will be helped.

There is no textbook "how to" when it comes to engagement, or the right step to take to begin to get involved. At the core of it all is the innate drive, the fire to want to make a difference, *somehow*. I did it by volunteering for causes and political campaigns that I felt were making a difference I wanted to see. I did it by learning by doing, by seeing a cause that spoke to me and working my way humbly from the bottom up to understand the issue and stay involved to gain experience around causes I cared about. I joined the boards of smaller local organizations to learn how to be involved in governance, and lead causes and organizations. From smaller roles and opportunities come bigger ones. I now serve on the boards of the ACLU National and the New Jersey ACLU. These organizations are changing the Draconian laws and policies that would have helped my father. It may be too late to help his case, but to be in leadership at an organization leading the way for prison reform is gratifying. It feels like justice. Justice for others is justice for me.

I also now work at the mothers and families advocacy group, MomsRising, where I also have worked on mass incarceration reform, addressing the very same issues that plagued my family.

My son, Zakir was born in 2015, a few years after my

father's release. We named him after my father. I did this in hopes that this time around, the name could be given a new chance, new opportunities. In the broken American dreams of his grandparents, these opportunities were never realized. I want to be there to ensure that he and all our children: black, white, brown, undocumented or documented, cisgender, transgender or non binary, LGBQ or straight, have a better chance for success and the opportunity to lead a happy, dignified life. I hope you will join me to help achieve this. Do it for yourself, do it for your kids, do it for your community, but more than anything, just do it.

Nadia is the Maternal Justice Campaign Director for the national mothers and families advocacy group, MomsRising, where she heads their work on mass incarceration, police reform and maternal health issues. She is the co-founder of the Bangladeshi American Women's Development Initiative (BAWDI), a grassroots organization that aims to empower, connect and organize Bangladeshi American women and girls in NJ. She serves on the Board of Trustees of the American Civil Liberties Union – New Jersey (ACLU-NJ) where she is the board's Equity Officer. She serves on the Economic Development Commission and Mental Health Stigma Task Force in her town of Bloomingdale, NJ. She was previously Program Director at the Andrew Goodman Foundation, where she built, led and grew the Vote Everywhere program, focusing on making voting more systematically accessible for communities all around the country. She previously served on the national governing board of the National Asian Pacific American Women's Forum (NAPAWF). Nadia has a deep passion for connecting grassroots work to systemic change and reform and increasing the political involvement and representation of women and marginalized communities. Prior to her current work, Nadia organized inner-city minority youth in California, taught photojournalism classes to refugee girls and worked as a domestic violence advocate for South Asian women and families.

https://bawdi.wordpress.com/
twitter.com/Vivalanadia
https://medium.com/@Vivalanadia

INTRODUCTION

Politics in the United States has an ugly stigma associated with it. Most women I know have absolutely no interest in discussing politics. As in, they don't want to get into a nasty argument over whether the Republican or the Democrat is right or wrong-whether or not abortion should be legal, who should be allowed to stay in the country legally, and so on and so forth. This may not be the case for you–perhaps you live in a region or have just grown up in an environment that is more open. However, in the deep South, where I live, there are three things we learn early on are impolite to discuss–money, religion, and politics. But overall, it's fairly clear that we are inept as a society at having a discussion with people who come from differing viewpoints without getting really nasty, really fast.

We've done a real disservice to ourselves over time by not being more engaged and involved in the "dirty" world of politics. We've essentially crippled the conversation by not learning how to have civil discussions around the topics that impact all of us on a daily basis.

But there is a movement afoot. A movement of women now motivated by the reality of our current culture and society to stand up for ourselves, our beliefs, our safety, our children's well-being, and our rights. We are part of that movement. If you're reading this book, YOU are, or are about to become, part of the movement too.

As parents, we pretty much have an obligation to be involved, on some level.

Parenting is political. Period.

I don't know any way around it.

From the moment we wake up to the moment we go to bed, everything we do is impacted in one way, shape or form by politics. The chemicals allowed into our mattress and sheets is political. Our milk and breakfast cereal are regulated, the cost of the electricity to run our house… regulated. Gas prices, the safety requirements on our vehicles, seatbelt laws, school zone speeds… we haven't even gotten the kids to school yet, and you can see how many elements of our lives are impacted by laws and regulations.

So to think that we can completely avoid politics is not realistic.

As women, we have no choice anymore but to join the discussion. Many of us are now starting to realize that women's issues are intersectional. Meaning, whether we are white, brown, purple, Christian, Jewish, Muslim, educated or not, mother or not, straight or not, married or not – when we support the rights of one of these groups, all women benefit. We cannot fight for rights of just one group of women, we have to be part of the entire discussion.

We certainly have a choice on how much we get involved, what issues we stake our claim in, and whether we are a positive part of the discussion.

It is my opinion that getting involved has to be important. It has to be to us, especially as mothers. It has to be a priority for us to be engaged in the conversation. But not just screaming at each other; not spreading fake news, rather, actually getting educated on the topics and having real discussions with people.

Because it matters.

On a very small level, I recently saw a friend post that she'd achieved a big win for her children's elementary school. The schools are divided into an Upper and Lower campus, with a small area of road in between them in which the speed zone did not drop. But children walk between the two schools all the time. Additionally, there is a middle school less than a _ mile away. She petitioned to have the school speed zone enforced through the entire section for all three schools. And she won. She made a positive impact and a massive change, simply by getting involved in the discussion because she was worried about the safety of her children and others. She used her voice. She spoke up about an issue. She took the steps to go to the schools and the Department of Transportation. And now, the entire stretch between all three schools is safer because of her efforts.

On a much larger scale, consider organizations like Mothers Against Drunk Driving or Moms Demand Action, or Moms Rising. These came out of a response to a need that mothers took on because of personal tragedies and or shortfalls in society. Women, especially mothers, can move mountains when we get behind an issue together.

In 2020, we've been faced with so many types of issues. Things that have brewing for a long time, like the injustices against black men in our country. There's never a better time to learn about issues, to stand up for what is right, and to get educated on the topics we thought we understand, but maybe don't. As an example, implicit bias and how we can do better as an ally to people of color in our country. And then, how we teach our children about this topic as well.

These are the types of issues (and oh, so many more!) that parents have to be talking about, discussing, getting engaged in. What are our kids eating for lunch? What subjects are being taught? Why have they done away with physical education? Should teachers REALLY be carrying guns? Are the teachers getting paid enough? Are special needs children's issues being adequately addressed? Are we getting the resources we need from the district and state? Why are kids in 5th grade committing suicide? Is there a problem with bullying in the school and what are we doing about it? Is mental health an issue?

The list above is just a smattering of the issues we think about as parents. But not a single one of them should result in blood-boiling, name-calling arguments. Heated debates? OK. We're passionate. Passion and disrespect do not have to go hand-in-hand.

It's time to make talking about politics cool again. It's time to be involved. It's past time to teach our children that they can be involved, can make a difference, can discuss these topics, and it can be done in a manner that is not disrespectful or hateful. We do that by opening dialogue, getting to know each other, having conversations together.

We need to start demonstrating to our children that we can have civilized conversations, even when we disagree, and still accomplish big things, in a kind and loving manner.

Not all instances of being involved will be kind and loving... I think we all realize that. But, when confrontation arises, how can we respond differently?

KEY TERMS

There are some key terms and concepts we mention throughout this book.

We talk about advocacy. This is the act or process of supporting a cause or proposal: the act or process of advocating about or for something. I am known for my advocacy for maternal and infant health and policies surrounding those topics.

I have coined my own term around this for mothers who are heavily involved in advocacy. I call us "momvocates" and we have a verb form as well... we "momvocate". As the mother of a micro preemie who spent 12 weeks in the NICU, and a son who has ADHD, I have learned very well what it takes to momvocate as I've navigated the medical and health care system. It ain't easy. If you carry the title of momvocate, you've earned it.

We talk about activism. This is the practice of taking vigorous action, or campaigning, with the goal of bringing about political or social change.

I like the Wikipedia definition of activism which states: Activism consists of efforts to promote, impede, direct, or intervene in social, political, economic, or environmental reform with the desire to make changes in society.

It's that desire to make positive reform that is usually the driving force behind most activists.

Activism can be further broken down into Social Activism – organizing specifically to bring about social change.

Social change refers to any significant alteration of behavior patterns and cultural values and norms. These changes happen over time and result in long-term consequences and changes in society. The legalization of marijuana is an example of social change.

Social Justice - equal access to wealth, opportunities, and privileges within a society. Leveling the playing field, if you will.

Many activists now describe themselves as Social Justice Warriors.

Social Justice Warrior (SJW): an individual who promotes socially progressive views, including feminism, civil rights, and multiculturalism, as well as identity politics.

This has been a term used negatively (and still is by some people) but women lately have been using it to describe themselves in their calls to action. When we use the term in this book, we are using it with respect and honor.

Getting involved.

I get it. You're overwhelmed. And perhaps a little scared to jump in.

Oh my goodness, do I understand! I am consistently overcommitted and overwhelmed! I know when I had 3 young ones 5 and under, I would not have been going to the State House to meet with representatives or attending meetings or doing anything outside of the house! This book is meant to demonstrate that there are so many ways you can get involved, and they don't all involve a lot of time or money.

This book is a collection of very diverse essays from

moms who have received the call to be involved socially and/or politically. The reasons they got involved all vary, but the common thread is that something happened to them or someone they care about or they saw a need and wanted to find a better solution than what existed. They began advocating for their cause, speaking up, and taking part in the process of making real and lasting change. Many of the mothers do it for their children. To make the world a better place for their children. Or if the reason they are involved existed prior to having children, they are involving their children and showing them the way to be Tiny Activists too. Children learn what is modeled for them, and if we want them to grow up to be adults that are involved in process, we have to show them the how and the why.

Throughout the book you'll learn about the motivations for involvement in social and political change, and simple things that you can do, right in your home, to be part of the movement. We've got suggestions, ideas, activities, and resources to help you as you consider how to get involved.

So, where do you fit in with all of this? What role do you want to play? Keep reading... and we'll help you answer those questions.

Alexa Bigwarfe

PART I:
A CALL TO ADVOCACY AND/OR ACTIVISM...

In this section, you'll read about why we got involved in our causes.

Getting involved is deeply personal. In these essays, our writers were called to service for different reasons, but a common thread runs through those reasons—the impetus to get involved was born out of a desire to make the world better for their children, to right a wrong, to seek a positive change that would have lasting effects for not just our families, but all families. Maybe one of these will resonate with you?

USE YOUR VOICE AND GET INVOLVED!
ALEXA BIGWARFE

At the age of 11 years old, as a 5th grader, I was held up at gunpoint at my bus stop. We didn't live in an exceptionally shady area, we were not being robbed. This gun was held by an unstable 16-year-old boy who was threatening to kill his sister, my classmate. She was standing next to me at the bus stop, and as a result, I had a gun pointed in my direction.

The gun belonged to his father and this boy had taken it from their home.

Thankfully, the bus came along, and he ran off. The cops later found him, at school, with the loaded gun.

This story could have ended in any number of ways, none of them positive, and I'm so grateful that I'm here to tell the story.

But this event changed me. For the next several years, I contemplated going to law school so that I could play a role in gun reform. I was only a 5th grader, and I could see there was a problem with our access to guns. And that was in 1988, long before school shootings became the issue that they are today.

I never pursued the law degree or the life in advocacy for gun control because I was afraid. I had a dream that I would be killed if I went this route, so fear stopped me from moving forward. But it stayed in the back of mind.

I followed other dreams and paths. We moved to Germany where my father was stationed with the military, and I fell in love with all things European. When I went to college, I decided to pursue a degree in international relations. I found a whole department of people interested in political science, and those were great days! Eventually I went into the military myself to pursue global peacekeeping actions.

Life went on. I got married, I started having kids. I got busy as a working mom. I always enjoyed discussing politics even though usually no one around me had any interest. I volunteered here and there on different campaigns but was never deeply involved.

And then, personal tragedy struck. My 3rd pregnancy came with a surprise. Identical twin girls! Who soon developed a frightening disease of the placenta called Twin-to-Twin-Transfusion Syndrome (TTTS). Without going into all of the details, they were born very sick, 10 weeks early, and one of them, my daughter Kathryn, passed away when she was 2 days old. Our surviving daughter, Charis, spent 12 weeks in the Neonatal Intensive Care Unit (NICU).

Over the next several months and years, I would learn how difficult our healthcare system is to navigate, how pathetic our laws and protections are for pregnant women, maternity care, maternity leave... how lacking our social policy and public policy still remain for women and children, how disappointing our health insurance program is, and what life is like trying to raise a special needs baby.

I began advocating for maternal and infant care, for more advances in neonatal research and development, and for programs that help pregnant women and babies.

I found my voice on a topic that resonated strongly because my world had come to a complete and total stop due to the shortfalls in our system. I watched other NICU mothers return to work shortly after delivering their babies because they wanted to save their leave time for when their baby returned home from the NICU. That is, if they were even lucky enough to have some type of maternity leave.

My heart continues to break at our high rates of pregnancy and infant mortality, as well as deaths of mothers during or shortly after childbirth. It continues to astonish me that in a country as grand as ours, we carry some of the highest mortality rates and the lowest amount of support or paid leave or healthcare programs.

I'm like many mothers out there. Something happened to us, or our children, that ignited a spark that was probably there for a long time... but we didn't know what to do about it. Then, once we had a reason we couldn't ignore, we took action. Maybe it's through volunteering or bringing awareness to topics, calling our elected officials, or raising money for a solution to a problem. There is such a wide array of activities that can be done to help find solutions to the many issues we face in our society. But the biggest step is the first one – deciding to get involved.

There are so many ways to get involved, and to show your children how to do it as well. One of the biggest things that I have taken on, and involve the entire family in, is our advocacy and fundraising efforts with the March of Dimes. The March of Dimes is the number one global organization for research and funding to determine the causes of prematurity, help women have healthy pregnancies, and develop cures for diseases and birth defects. Most of the advances in neonatal care have come from programs, funding, and research from the March of Dimes. I had heard of the March of Dimes but had no understanding of its mission, until we were in the NICU with our daughter. We got involved immediately and raised a lot of money in just 2 months. We participated in our first walk only one month after our daughter came home from the NICU. The following year, we were the Ambassador family for our region. My daughter and I traveled all over our area of the state, speaking to different groups about our experience and why raising money for the March of Dimes is so important.

I traveled to Washington, DC for an advocacy day, meeting with elected officials so that they would understand why supporting different bills and proposals are so important to mothers and babies. Over 6 years later, I still am a strong advocate for this organization and for the cause as a whole. And now, I'm starting to branch out into other ways I can help women and children. I'd love nothing more than to be a part of passing a national paid maternity leave program and paid sick time off for all workers, regardless of working status or state. There is so much data to show how productive workers can be when they have these programs and protections.

My children are all also actively involved as advocates for the March of Dimes and healthy babies. They each raise money for the annual walk. Charis has raised over $1000 and we set that as an annual goal for her. From the time they have been itty bitty, they have collected coins for Team Charis and Kat so that they can help babies. We attend the walk every year and we talk about why it's important to be part of events like that, to be part of the solution for the problems in our society and community.

There is much work to be done. There are so many programs and initiatives I want to be a part of. I know I can't do it all, so I start where I'm most passionate, and I do what I can. Sometimes, it's just sending out emails to ask for donations. Sometimes it's writing blog posts to bring awareness to my cause. Sometimes, it's just talking to my kids about our role in society and why it matters.

Find what it is you're most passionate about trying to solve. I guarantee you, there is an organization that needs your help, and will take what you've got, even if you don't have a lot of time or energy.

You've got this!

Alexa Bigwarfe is a loud advocate for those without a voice. She is a USA Today Best Selling Author, an author coach, and a publisher. She coaches others through the self-publishing process at writepublishsell.com. She started blogging as an outlet for her grief after the loss of one of her twin daughters to Twin to Twin Transfusion Syndrome (TTTS) and now uses the blog to advocate for those without a voice. She is also the founder of LoseThe-Cape.com, and is the editor and publisher of the Lose the Cape! series. The mother of three wildlings, Alexa spends her free time coming up with ways to try to save the world from her home in Columbia, SC and drags her children along for the ride.

WE'VE GOT TO HOLD THE LINE
BELLAMY SHOFFNER

A fortnight before Trayvon Martin was murdered, I gathered with friends and family around my six-month-old firstborn, a mini-cake, and wrapped gifts and cards celebrating his first half-birthday. I was immersed in the weary bliss of new motherhood and had no inkling that just two weeks later, my world would lose its footing along with that of every mother to every Black son in the United States of America. Trayvon's death was infinitely more than a media sensation. Leaps and bounds beyond a story to be told and long forgotten, it was an alarm sounding to let us all know we had to rise up in hopes of keeping our Black children from being gunned down like a hunter's prey.

And then, the murders kept happening... and kept happening. One by one another beloved son or daughter became unironically immortalized in the form of a hashtag while their parents and community grieved. Children ripped from their families at the hands of police and vigilantes. Staying alive as a Black person in America felt like a compulsory playing round of Russian roulette. Was there any way to increase our odds of survival?

Two years later, I gave birth to another baby boy. From his initial breath, he radiated an undeniable fierceness that let me know he would always challenge me to be adaptable and solution-minded, he would require radical problem-solving and intense protection. He would demand my fierceness in deference to his. This child's feisty nature served as a wake-up call—yet another alarm, this one more personal, reminding me that my darling boys will one day be vocal and bold and brilliant and independent, walking through life without the protective shield of their parents. My boys will eventually be on their own moving through the world as teens, and later, adult men. With brown skin making them a threat to America, the targets on the backs of my sons will grow as they do.

The truth terrified me.

My concern prompted the question: How could I help in a concrete and meaningful way? (This is a question I urge everyone to ask themselves every day they are able.) I'd weighed my options, within the confines of my reality: resources, my health, and my talents. My answer was to avoid the trap of blogging to fuel mommy wars and instead write to provoke transformative thought, demand inclusive parenting, and drive awareness of social and cultural divides.

After freelancing for some time, I started Hold the Line: a digital magazine dedicated to examining the many intersections where parenthood + social justice collide. In addition to the magazine, Hold the Line is also an organization that serves as an online discussion group, hosts an annual retreat, free community events, workshops, and an ongoing food drive. Social entrepreneurship is a priority and we are committed to giving

10% of profits to organizations whose work aligns with our goal of being champions of social equity.

My goal with starting Hold the Line was to foster a community in which we tell our stories, but also a place where we can help others learn how they can be champions for equity and inclusivity. We even provide activities that parents, and other caregivers, can do with their children to support social change.

One of the key elements of Hold the Line and the piece that is truly imperative to the mission of reframing closely held but problematic beliefs lies in the personal connections we are helping to make. By prioritizing both truth and kindness, we are able to connect with readers and community members with a foundation of productive conversation. If we're having discussions like this, it's not always going to be easy. When you are challenged to question your biases and misconceptions and forced to check your privilege, it can get uncomfortable. I am uncomfortable when I'm hit with new information even though I have, without a doubt, made it my job to know and do better. If you can't handle the awkward and heavy gut feeling of finding out you were wrong, you cannot be an agent of change. While there are some folks with problematic beliefs that no level of discussion may change their minds, those who are willing to sit with uncomfortable truths and learn and grow with the content are able to grow from our mutually beneficial community.

My instincts told me to use my writing to demand equity for all and to amplify the voices of others who are doing the same. Together, we can improve the likelihood that my sons are allowed to grow up to be teenagers, who grow up to be men, who are able to live in peace. Together we can ensure the disgraceful unearned targets they carry upon their backs are replaced by the freedom to live unencumbered by hate.

Will you join us and help us Hold the Line?

Bellamy Shoffner is a writer and creator of Hold the Line, a digital magazine committed to exploring the intersection of parenthood and social-justice. She looks forward to launching HTL Champions a multi-offering initiative with a continued committed to raising champions for change. Bellamy's freelance work has been enjoyed by hundreds of thousands of readers through sites like The Establishment, Scary Mommy, elephant journal, For Harriet, Mamalode and other reputable publications. Her work has also been republished by Narratively, Everyday Feminism, and HuffPost. In addition to writing, Bellamy is partner to a supportive husband and mother to two clever, energetic children. She resides with her family in Charlottesville, Virginia.

Websites:
www.hellobellamy.co (this is the site that links most of my personal writing)
www.htlmagazine.com

Social Media:
https://www.facebook.com/hellobellamyco/
https://www.instagram.com/weholdtheline/
https://twitter.com/hellobellamy

IF WE DON'T DO IT, WHO WILL?
HEATHER VICKERY

I remember sitting in the car, right after the 2016 election, with my then 12-year-old daughter, Olivia. She turned to me, afraid, and said, "I am not worried about me. I know that I am a white, straight, girl and I have a lot of privilege—but I am worried about you."

She was worried about me because I am a lesbian. She knew that the new administration might not take kindly to the LGBTQ+ community, that our hard-earned rights were in danger.

I smiled and took her hand. I thanked her because she is kind and thoughtful and smart. Yes. She is a white, straight, girl and yes, she has a lot of privilege because of it. But because Olivia is still only a child and her scope of understanding is limited by default, I said, "Let me tell you all of the reasons you should be scared for yourself!"

I rattled off the list: women's rights, gun violence, potential war, environmental concerns … the list was long and she was shocked. As smart as she is, she had not figured out just how much politics and government could affect her life. She nodded, absorbed it and asked a lot of questions. I did my best to answer those questions. I deeply believe that the ability to ask thoughtful questions and have them answered is a key ingredient in being, and raising, activists.

SO WHAT IS PRIVILEGE?

We talk a lot about privilege in our household. We talk about the importance of using our privilege to help others when we can. But what does that even mean? And how do we teach it to our children? Privilege is knowing that you have a right to go to school, to eat three meals a day, and have clean food. My privilege means I can return an item to The Gap, without a receipt, without being accused of stealing it. It means that, for the most part, when I say something, people believe me. Assumptions are made about my honesty, trustworthiness, and intelligence level exclusively based on my skin color. It would be foolish for me to deny these privileges and it would be deadly for me not to use them to help others whenever possible.

One lesson I have learned in my life is that many people are resistant to "learning" from those who are different than they are. I don't really believe it is a lack of desire or interest (at least in most cases) but it feels uncomfortable and confusing for some people. This is why I believe that, because of my white privilege, I am duty and honor bound to call other white people out on their "ism's."

There is no greater gift than "in the moment feedback." (Side note, I believe this is true in almost all cases, about everything.) That may mean telling a family member it isn't okay to say, "That guy looks like a fruit," because it is presumptuous and insulting. Or reminding someone that wearing a specific outfit does not indicate intelligence level or value. No one has the right to stand in judgement of how a person grieves a loss, celebrates a win, or walks down the street. We must have difficult conversation with people who are "like" us because, in most cases, they would not dream of having a conversation with someone different than them. While I am not an expert in this, my life experience and self-guided education tells me this behavior is often not intentional. If you ask most people if they were willing to have a conversation with someone of a different race, religion or sexual orientation, most of them would say yes. This isn't about willingness—it is about the unconscious bias we all experience. Yes, ALL of us! Unconsciously, we gravitate to people who are like us. It feels safer and it is much easier to have someone you identify with give you constructive criticism and education than someone who is different than you.

When I was in middle and high school, the majority of my friends were black or Jewish. I don't really think I realized it then, but it is the truth. I was fortunate enough to go to a very diverse school (even in the heart of Indiana) and be exposed to people, religions, and lifestyles that were vastly different from my own. The gifts this opportunity presented me are endless and ever-present but the most prevalent was that I was constantly in conversation with people who were not like me. It removed the fear and stigma of "other" from my life.

Back in those days we used to say we were "color blind". We truly believed that was good. Not seeing color or race as an obstacle had to be good, right? We were all equal, right? Um, no. I have since learned the danger in this thought process. By not seeing someone's skin color, you strip them of the right to their history and their uniqueness. This train of thought is like telling a rape victim that "not all men are bad". It diminishes a personal truth. It lumps everyone together and it is dangerous. It is so much better to see and honor the differences in all people, to talk about race and culture not as a "strange thing" but simply as a reality. Again, I say ask questions. Learn more about a person and their story. Make an effort to understand how their lives have unfolded and about their fears and hopes.

That said, one of the most important lessons I have learned just in the last few years is that it is not someone else's responsibility to educate me. It is no one else's responsibility to teach me why they are equal or educate me on their struggles. It must be my own responsibility to educate myself and my children on the reality of privilege. The example I gave about returning an item to The Gap without a receipt just happened a few weeks ago. We received a gift that didn't fit properly and went to return it, without a receipt. I was given store credit and not questioned at all, but I had to wonder, if I had been a person of color, would that have been my experience? I chose to talk to my daughter about it. I wanted her to understand that our privilege likely played a powerful role in returning that item. We must not take things like this for granted and we must remain aware.

The river runs deep.

When I was a child my mother used to call me a "save-the-whales" kind of girl. I wanted to help everyone I could. I couldn't stand to see someone being hurt, marginalized, or undervalued. I was never afraid of speaking out or stepping up. Once

I became a parent, the desire to be even more of an activist grew. These little girls are always watching me. They are doing what I do—the good and the bad. All kids imitate their parents in some capacity. The importance of raising socially conscious and aware children weighs heavily on me but it does not weigh me down—it motivates me. It encourages me and gives me purpose and hope.

My daughters are growing up in two homes. One with me and my partner, and one with their father (where he is severely outnumbered by our four little girls). This means they are already not living the standard, traditional "American lifestyle". They are also fortunate to live in a community that is extremely diverse in just about every way possible. Based on these factors, my kids already have a different perspective than a good portion of the nation. We live in a community of love and acceptance (at least most of the time) and know the difference between acceptance and tolerance. Tolerance cannot ever be the goal as it is by definition "the ability or willingness to tolerate something, in particular the existence of opinions or behavior that one does not necessarily agree with." It is not enough to tolerate. We must accept that which is "an agreement with or belief in an idea or opinion." Beyond this, we embrace others and fight with them.

I am constantly blown away by my daughters' ability to respect and validate someone who is non-binary or transgender. They can so easily and quickly alter their language and pronouns to make the other person comfortable, to show them, right off the bat, that they are safe. My daughters have a deep understanding that not every person identifies as the gender they were assigned at birth. I would like to take all of the credit for this, but I am not sure I can. I have laid the foundation for my children to be able to ask questions, to not take things at face value and dig deeper, to be in conversation—and they do it! I lead them down the path but they have to do the work themselves. They question me (sometimes to my frustration!) and their father. They even challenge grandparents or family members when they see or hear something they don't understand or agree with. They question their teachers and administrators. They have learned not to accept "status quo" if something seems unbalanced. It takes a lot of guts to do this, especially outside of our cozy little bubble. They may look at me as a guide in their education as activists but they are doing the hard work all on their own and it makes all the difference.

ALL FIGHTS ARE MY FIGHT

We have some standard statements in our home. "All bodies are beautiful," "Black Lives Matter" (and in so saying, it does not mean that your life doesn't matter), "All fights must be my fight."

I am a divorced mom of four little girls. I am also a lesbian in a long-term domestic partnership. My partner, Bernadette, and I were in Las Vegas the night of the 2016 election. We stopped and bought two bottles of champagne and planned to celebrate, but as the night wore on, it became clear that things were going very wrong. The next morning, numb and in shock, we talked about getting married. We were, after all in Vegas. We talked about it because, all of the sudden, the fear of losing our right to marry seemed very real. We decided that decisions made out of fear never end well and we should wait for the right time. We were determined to fight for our rights.

This is an easy fight to take on. But not all fights always are. That last part of our motto, "All fights must be my fight"—that is the one that I work on the hardest. The idea that simply because something might not affect you directly (or at least you may not easily notice how you will be affected) doesn't mean you don't stand up and fight the fight. When I had that conversation in the car with Olivia I knew that this message was getting through to her. She was worried about me. She was worried about LGBTQ+ rights. She was ready to stand up and fight for this despite it not being her fight. All fights must be everyone's fight.

I am reminded of a poem by Martin Niemoller. The gist of the poem is that, if you sit on the sidelines while other people's rights are taken away, eventually, no one will be around to support you when your own rights are threatened. The time to speak up and get involved is now!

So, I teach my girls: All fights are our fight.

Last spring, when students were walking out of their classrooms in protest of gun violence, all three of my school aged daughters participated in the walk out. In nearly all of these cases, I learned about my kids' participation after they happened. I was A-OK with this because I never want my girls to ask permission before doing what they think is right. At first, these walk outs were fairly easy. There was no real risk involved and, I am sure on some level, it was the "cool" thing to do. The administrators emailed us and said they would be allowed to leave class and they would suffer no consequences. While I appreciated their supporting the kids right to speak out and protest, there didn't seem to be much of a risk or a lesson here. Yes, these protests felt good and brought the kids together as a community but the thing about protests is, they only really work when there is something risked. Consider Selma or Stonewall. There must be a consequence risked for it to have an impact.

The day before the third walk out, one of my daughters came to me concerned. She had a math test scheduled to take place during the protest. If the teacher would not let her retake the test, what was she to do? This is the moment I had been waiting for. This is where the rubber meets the road, as they say.

Never being one to answer these questions for my children, I asked her "I don't know. What do you think you should do?" "I'll probably go anyway," she said. This led to a powerful conversation about consequences and risks. It is easy to protest, march, canvas, and put signs up when there is nothing at stake but what happens when you miss a math test and your A goes to a B? Or when you get hateful words strewn at you when you are marching? Or when you get arrested? In the end, we agreed, if it was worth the fight, it had to be worth the risk.

ACTIVISM HAS MANY FACES

One thing I have discovered is that there are a lot of different ways to be an activist and to raise socially conscious children. Yes, there is marching and protesting. I took my daughters with me to the Women's March and, yes, I was scared. I was cautious for their safety and leery of a government that might retaliate for our presence- but we went because staying home was not an option. Sitting on the sidelines is not an option. Silence is equivalent to the crimes we are fighting so hard against. But there are other ways to be an activist and an overall good human. Topping this list, for me, is kindness and conversation. I have tough conversations with my girls about race so that their friends of color don't have to educate my little white girls (it is not their friends' job- it's my job). We talk about those that are differently abled and how we can best advocate for them, but also the importance of treating them as equals with kindness and respect. And I do my best not to just talk to them, but to show them. Actions always speak louder than words and silence... well, *silence is deadly.*

On the topic of kindness and equality: three of my daughters attend the same summer camp. A family that we are very close to has two daughters in the same camp. One of their daughters is differently abled and wheelchair bound. She is not at the same mental level as her twin sister or my kids, but Abbey is a pretty amazing kid. She and I are good friends. We get each other, it seems, and as such I make a point of stopping by to say hello and give her a hug each day.

Last week Abbey's father pulled me aside to say, "thank you". When I inquired as to why, he said, "Your kids are so kind to Abbey. They are truly good friends to her and make it a point to include her in their daily conversations and activities."

I smiled and said "We all love Abbey. We get as much out of it as she does."

And he said, "Behavior like that is learned, it comes from the top. So, thank you."

I sat with that for quite a while. My children are each their own person. They are strong willed, independent thinkers. They know right from wrong and good from bad. I never had to ask them to socialize with Abbey; they did it of their own free will. But it is true that acceptance of anyone or anything that is "different" from you is learned behavior. Just as the opposite is true.

I am reminded of a conversation I had with another daughter a couple of years ago. Lying in bed one night she asked me, "Momma, people who don't think like me, are they bad? Or did they just learn something different than I did?" These are not the types of questions I want to answer for my kids, so I said, "I don't know, what do you think?" "I think they just learned different things. But I want to talk to them about it. I want to know why they feel that way. I want to understand all sides."

My inner activist, proud momma was cheering inside as I calmly sat there and said, "Yes, I think that is the right answer." I sincerely believe in the importance of conversation. Being so deeply rooted in your own beliefs that you are not willing to talk to others about theirs and learn their motives and intentions is very dangerous. In fact, I would say it is the root of our issues as a nation. We have all dug our heels in and said, "If you don't think like me you are bad, and I won't talk to you". But that doesn't solve anything!

In this social media driven world, we feel like we are making a difference by clicking on something or sharing a link. It is not working. We have to be in the trenches and we must take our children with us. They should see the work and the result of the work first hand. I don't have the luxury of throwing my hands in the air and giving up. My children are watching and I need them to fight. I can't give up because they can't give up.

Being an activist can be loud, but it can also be quiet. There is time for all of it and in order to make it to the finish line (if such a thing exists) we must remember to slow down and take a deep breath now and then. We cannot run ourselves so hard that we break down and have nothing left to give. Consider activism like playing a wind instrument. If you play consistently, without stopping to breathe, you sound crappy and eventually cannot continue and no one wants to listen to you. But a good, deep breath and you can play for a very long time and create raving fans in the process.

All this to say, I believe the most powerful way to raise socially conscious (activist if you will) children is to teach them to talk to people, to approach situations with kindness and an open mind, to fight for the rights of those both alike and different than themselves. To truly see those differences and to honor them (none of this "color blind" business—that is a dangerous way to think), to raise them up to the light and breathe life into them.

As humans, I believe it is our obligation to love each other. To lift each other up, support each other, fight alongside and for one another. If we don't do it, who will?

Heather Vickery is an award-winning entrepreneur, business owner, and transformational life and business coach. But Heather isn't just a savvy businesswoman _ she's an inspiration. The founder of Vickery and Co., Heather is a featured expert on achieving an authentic and meaningful life and designing your own roadmap for balance and success.

A mother of four, Heather's world turned upside down after a major life transformation and divorce, suddenly, she had the freedom to be her most authentic self. She discovered that this same authenticity empowered her with the confidence she needed to repair, rebuild, and reach her life's vision and goals. Today, Heather leverages her entrepreneurial skills and expertise to coach individuals towards greater personal and professional fulfillment. Through her story of personal bravery, perseverance, and resilience, Heather inspires audiences and empowers attendees with the tools they need to live bold and meaningful lives. A strong believer in strengthening her community, Heather also serves as the Vice President on the school board for The Children's School and as Vice President on the Board of Directors for the About Face Theatre. She is obsessed Hamilton An American Musical and loves to travel. Heather is also the host of The Brave Files Podcast.

TWITTER: @vickeryandco
INSTAGRAM: @vickeryandco
FACEBOOK: https://www.facebook.com/VickeryandCo and https://www.facebook.com/thebravefilespodcast
LINKEDIN: https://www.linkedin.com/in/heather-vickery/
YOUTUBE: https://www.youtube.com/heathervickery
PINTEREST: https://www.pinterest.com/vickeryco

TIKKUN OLAM

NANCY CAVILLONES

Tikkun Olam.

Loosely translated from the Hebrew, it means, To Heal the World.

Tikkun Olam is a basic tenet of Judaism. In Judaism, we practice this through volunteerism and serving others in the community. My father took this seriously, volunteering his time in the Jewish community. He served on committees and boards. He delivered meals on Thanksgiving morning to the homebound. He gave the elderly rides to Shabbat services. Time, I learned, is just as important as money. Volunteering is a quiet way to make a local and direct impact on the community. Volunteering is a facet of social activism.

My favorite Hebrew song includes the line, "hineh ma-tov umanaim shevet achim gam yachad."

"See how good and pleasant it is for brothers (and sisters) to dwell together in harmony."

Volunteerism goes hand in hand with social action. For us to dwell together in harmony, we each have to be personally touched. Yes, we can march with our signs, we can hit that donate button, we can sign petitions, we can vote. But in all that "WE", there has to be an "I" and a "You". What am I doing every day to make an impact on a single person? What's the action that I am taking to move things ever forward? In Judaism, we call this the mitzvah. What's the good deed I am performing?

We heal the world, person by person. As a person, I have the power to be part of a solution, no matter what the cause. My mother also demonstrated this for me. When I was a kid, I volunteered with my mom at our local food co-op because I thought it was fun. I didn't realize at the time that I was helping to sustain a source of healthy foods for the community—I was part of the food justice movement and I didn't even know it. I just liked helping people, and I loved the co-op. As an adult, that carried over into volunteering at the food pantry with my temple's Sisterhood.

I have a vivid memory of marching in front of Planned Parenthood in downtown Albany, NY with my mother. We were demonstrating in support of access to reproductive rights, and though I might not have fully understood all that lay at stake, my mother did, and I followed her lead. Sometimes, a louder voice is needed to make an impact.

Jews consider ourselves problem-solvers. We want to make things right. Our sense of justice comes from a long history, both biblical and contemporary, of repression, being passed over, subjected to genocide, victims of subtle and not-so-subtle discrimination. To fight is to survive as a people. We fight with words, with ideas, with dreams. We fight with our time and our energy, and yes, sometimes, our money.

When the Syrian refugee crisis came to a head, my sister

and I were called to action. The Jewish people are no strangers to refugee status. My own great-grandfather came to America to escape the pogroms, violent massacres that targeted Jews, and ravaged Eastern Europe. The best action is direct action. We joined a group in Connecticut called DARA, Danbury Area Refugee Assistance, and helped to resettle a family of five from Syria. Five lives are just as valuable as hundreds of thousands of lives, and we were able to help those five lives, so different from ours and yet, not so different.

But the best part to me was that my children were part of this process. They helped us welcome the family, gave the children a gift of toys, and experienced tremendous Syrian hospitality. They knew about the Syrian refugee crisis but meeting this family made it real for them, a memory they will keep forever.

My children watch me the same way I watched my parents. They see me getting out in the community, dedicating myself to the causes that matter most to me. They get a taste of social action in Religious School, making sandwiches for the soup kitchen or participating in our temple's annual Mitzvah Day, a day full of mitzvahs. Jewish children learn about mitzvahs at an early age. The small mitzvahs—saying please and thank you. The bigger mitzvahs—collecting food for the needy. They all matter. They shape our children into adults that do good things, that serve their communities, that use their voices for people whose voices aren't being heard.

When we introduce our children to the concept of volunteerism and social action, we plant the seed for future harmony and justice. It's a cliché but it's true—children are our greatest hope for the future. But they need us to shepherd them, to lead, to act. To show them that a single mitzvah can be a balm for a single hurt, that a whole lot of mitzvahs can heal the world.

If you're not sure where to begin with your own family, start with social action as a value. Say, "in our family, we VALUE helping others, we VALUE giving back, we VALUE speaking up for the disenfranchised." Then, take it one step further—put your time and energy where your mouth is. Get involved through your place of worship, if you have one. Contact your school's PTA—most have a community service committee. Call the animal shelter or the local food pantry and find out how you and your children can help. There are so many organizations that need and would love your help.

Nancy Cavillones enjoys taking the scenic route, forcing her kids to appreciate nature, and spending time in New York City by herself in a desperate attempt to recapture her college days. Nancy recently relocated to Northern California with her family, where she hopes sweater weather exists. She is Managing Editor of Lose the Cape and co-host of the Lose The Cape podcast. http://therealnani.com

"NEVER DOUBT THAT A SMALL GROUP OF THOUGHTFUL, COMMITTED, CITIZENS CAN CHANGE THE WORLD. INDEED, IT IS THE ONLY THING THAT EVER HAS."

—MARGARET MEAD

ACCIDENTAL ACTIVIST
MASON AID

The meetings start with the leaders screaming "AYYYYY!" at the top of their lungs and the teens echo in a chorus and begin to settle down. "Alright friends, you know the drill, Name, Pronouns, News!" We go around the circle and hear about everyone's relationships, life issues, and small news they want to share with the group.

"My name is Mason, I use they/their pronouns, and I am an accidental activist."

It surprised me when others started referring to me as an activist, because it's not what I set out to be. This word still sits strangely with me. I didn't set out to become this person, this journey simply led me here. The belief that I HAVE to speak out on behalf of my community, on behalf of the teens I work with, compelled me into a position where I am being sought out for my knowledge.

The journey to activism started out in a fairly unexpected manner. In 2012, I was single and depressed, having just ended a three-year relationship. Surfing okCupid, I found someone who interested me and I messaged her. We began chatting and as I got to know her I found out that she ran an LGBTQ teen group called Prism in our college town. I was (and still am) smitten and wanted to get involved immediately. "Not yet," she said, not wanting to put the teens through a possible break up. When the other coordinator was unable to make a meeting, it became necessary for me to come (Prism's official boundaries require two adults because some people suck).

When I set foot into The Center Project building that evening, I had no idea the course of my life was about to change. Cliché, I know, but also completely true. I was depressed or manic at the time, bipolar disorder rearing its ugly head. Thankfully I found a new sense of stability in the relationship I had just started with my now wife, Hilary. I was in college studying sociology with a vague desire to go to graduate school for... something. Twenty-six years old and finally coming out from the weight of years of mental health issues while slowly settling into myself and my queer identity, I found purpose in working with these teens.

My work with Prism started small. At the first meetings, there were two adults and two teens, a small group where we really got to know each other. I had the privilege of learning about these kids and how they found the self-awareness and courage to come out at such a young age. Showing up every week and talking while making shrinky-dinks; simply being there in the building was really all I did. Slowly though, it grew. Two teens became four, which became ten, which became 25-30 a week.

My involvement in community issues also expanded. I was asked to be on a local committee to consider high school graduation rates in the community. This committee was made up of many people who were involved in the lives of high schoolers in the community; teachers, administrators, and non-profit workers. I was amazed to be included in a room with people who I saw as change-makers—people who were actively making a difference in the lives of people in our community.

And in the midst of it, there I was. Me. A punk queer from rural Missouri whose voice was being heard for what seemed like the first time. I was an expert on something simply for living my life and being there for the teens I cared about so tremendously.

I was asked to do a presentation for a local high school and figured "Why not?" So, I prepped and planned and researched and presented; and I realized I had found something which lit a fire in me I had never experienced before. I knew I wanted to do more. I wanted to educate.

I realized in a way I hadn't before that most people don't intend to be offensive, they honestly just don't know better. Perhaps that belief comes from my own homophobic past, having grown up in a conservative Christian environment, I internalized the belief that I was doomed to hell because of who I am attracted to. Perhaps it is simply a byproduct of being someone who believes the best about everyone.

Learning and expanding my views is an important element of my life, and I'm always looking for ways to grow as a person. So, I read and I listen to podcasts. My wife got me hooked on an amazing podcast called "Raise Your Hand Say Yes," and I began to think about what I wanted to raise my hand to, what life I wanted to say yes to. This led to me starting my own blog on which I share about my experiences as a queer person with bipolar disorder. Eventually, I faced my inner fears and shared the blog on Facebook. People actually liked it! I found myself writing more and speaking more; taking every opportunity I had to educate people on the experiences of queer people, especially those in the transgender and non-binary community. As I continued to put my beliefs into action, a word started to be used for me which I wasn't entirely comfortable with at the beginning.

"Yeah, my friend Mason is an LGBTQ activist."

Yes. I am an activist, I guess. I am a different kind of activist though; I'm not throwing paint on people wearing fur, I'm not chaining myself to a tree. Honestly, I've only been to one or two rallies because I have a small child at home, and they're always during naptime. Even though I can't attend every rally, I will never stop taking action. I will never stop speaking out and advocating for queer teens. I will share my story, I will share the stories of the teens I have worked with over the years; I will not sit back and let the people I love continue to be hurt.

And I will raise my daughter to know using her voice is one of the greatest privileges she has as well.

Mason Aid is an educator and advocate for diversity and inclusion focused on the LGBTQ community. They grew up on a small farm in rural Northeast Missouri and have since moved to the teeming metropolis of Columbia, Missouri. They got their start working with LGBTQ teens and found passion through this work. Seeing the experiences and lives of these amazing youth had a profound impact on Mason, and through their volunteer work they found opportunities training educators and social service providers. They have since grown those opportunities into a business working with online entrepreneurs to help others avoid the "accidental asshole" moment.

Mason loves spending time with her wife and baby, going on walks, cooking good food, and pretending to be a pretentious coffee snob. Find her at: www.themasonaid.com

www.instagram.com/masonaid

SHOWING UP SO MY DAUGHTER CAN RECOGNIZE HER PURPOSE AND RESILIENCE IN MAKING AN IMPACT IN THIS WORLD

DESIREE PETERKIN-BELL

I am a mother, a wife, and an entrepreneur. I strive to live a life driven by purpose. I haven't always gotten things right. For example, it took a shake to my core to reveal I had been creating brands for men in politics and their families, before even being fully present for my own. My life has come with many lessons, but the greatest lesson thus far for me has been to let my daughter see me be vulnerable, uncomfortable, fail and get right back up.

I have often been the youngest, brownest, only female at a decision-making table in politics and government for over 20 years. And trust me when I tell you, it has not been easy. Politics is a full contact sport. An industry often susceptible to people driven by ego, grandstanding and protecting their legacy, you can run against considerable roadblocks trying to make a difference and impact. But the obstacles and those tunneled-visioned opportunists I've run up against hasn't stopped my desire, or my drive to help change the world. Being driven by purpose and not position means that I operate to make an impact in the world and my community, and I'm driven by that every day. I don't chase titles, accolades or roles. I chase impact.

I wake up every day wanting my daughter's world to be better. I keep a journal of all the things I believe will help my daughter succeed in life. These are the issues I work on. Whether it's fighting for her safety in school or outside; marching to make sure she doesn't become a police brutality statistic; advocating for investments in clean water and climate change; encouraging investments in healthy food choices; lobbying for her right to choose what she can do with her body or when the time comes, making sure that she has the right to love and be with whoever she wants to be with, and most importantly that she can live the life promised to her under the constitution of these United States with certain inalienable Rights, that among these are Life, Liberty and the Pursuit of Happiness. This is why I work.

Throughout my career in government and politics, there have been a few who questioned why I was even at the table. The intersectionality of the hierarchies of race and gender speaks to the challenges that Black women face, both as women and as black people, in politics and in society as a whole. Some of the work that I have done and the people I have supported have put me in the crosshairs of injustice, hate and political pettiness. I don't hide any of these experiences from my daughter. I want her to know that when you do try to make an impact, you may come in contact with people and systems that may try to stop you- but you can't stop. You have to keep going.

In a world that is driven by a 24-hour news cycle, many of us are nervous about what alerts pop up on our phones. It can feel like the world has become so much more tense and scary. Turning on the television, you would think that we all hate each other, no place is safe, and things are at a stalemate in Washington, D.C. But perspective is key when we are trying to explain the world and the state of affairs to our children. My recommendation for parents trying to raise a child in a world that may seem a bit frightening at times is to:

1. Be open and honest. Share your feelings as well and don't deny that something, an event/tragedy actually occurred. In this day and age, kids can find information often in a context that supports their fears and not their hopes, via the internet or hearing about it in passing. It's better for children to get information, context, and facts from someone they trust.

2. The reality is that there is more good and there are more good people in this world than there are bad people and bad things happening.

3. The question I always ask my daughter after one of these talks is, what can you do to help? How can you make a difference tomorrow? And, the answer could simply be, being nice to someone who is different from them, smiling at the new kid in school or listening to their teacher.

In my work, my daughter Kaelyn has met (I have often had to bring her along with me to these meetings) congressional members, city council members, youth activists, governors, foreign leaders and presidents. Today, my daughter knows, even at her young age, she can speak truth to power and help to make an impact in her world. She and I have frequent conversations about her desire to ensure that young women know they can be in any room and use their voice. She has already begun to do this on her own at school, where she insisted after significant accounts of bullying were documented, that the school bring in and develop an anti-bullying curriculum so that students can feel safe.

I do the work because I want my daughter to know there are no limits to her vision of who she can be. My husband also knows what's at stake for our daughter's future and the necessity of seeing representation, believing in her own abilities and having confidence in who she can become.

I want young women of color, particularly black women, to know they have the power to make a change. The trials and tribulations of life and the severe insecurities of others can be a bit overwhelming. But you can't let the small-mindedness win. No one can take your power, you are a force to be reckoned with.

Desiree Peterkin Bell strives to identify, create, and leverage traditional and nontraditional media, and define strategies that work. Desiree Peterkin Bell is a strategist, brand builder and problem solver. In recognition of her efforts, Desiree has been honored as one of the industry's best and brightest by PR Week's "40 under 40"; as a 'Shorty Award' winner; by the Philadelphia Tribune as "One of Philadelphia's Most Influential African-American Women"; by Black Enterprise as a "triple threat", and by Philadelphia Business Journal as a "40 under 40" recipient.

Prior to establishing DPBell & Associates, Desiree Peterkin Bell served in two appointed positions for the City of Philadelphia and for former Mayor Michael A. Nutter: Director of Communications and Strategy, and City Representative. As Director of Communications she was responsible for creating and leading local, regional, national, international, traditional and non-traditional media strategies for the City of Philadelphia and Mayor Michael A. Nutter. She crafted the first-ever social media policy for the City of Philadelphia and built an award winning online presence for the City.

http://www.desireepeterkinbell.com/services/

BRING YOUR OWN CHAIR TO THE TABLE
CHOU HELLEGRA

A few years ago, I wanted to sign up my son for a preschool program in our community. I filled out the typical forms that often come along with such enrollment. On the form, I was genuine in my responses. One question asked if my child had any special needs. I shared my son's Autism diagnosis. Little did I know, that response would delay my son's acceptance into the program. A case manager finally reached out to the program on my behalf and discovered that the school determined that my son was not a good fit for the full-time program; they were concerned about being able to support a child with special needs.

Needless to say, I was livid and frustrated by a system that had written off my son without consulting me or meeting him. In my own work as a disability consultant, I hear stories like mine all the time. They range from the passive-aggressive, "Maybe another program would be more suitable," to the outright lie, "We're booked."

If only she had talked to me directly. She would've learned that her concerns, although valid, could be addressed. If she did not have the resources to support my kid in this educational environment, I would have connected her to the support available to her and to her agency. We had the resources to support this director and her staff.

This director did not ask how she could support my child; instead, she wrote my child off. The solution she offered did not consider what my child needed or what we needed as a family. How often are kids with attention deficit disorders, conduct disorders, developmental disabilities, and other conditions being written off by school administrators? Schools often take the easy way out, trying to make things easier for adults. We need to include the people that we're trying to help in the decisions that we make regarding their care. They need to be at the center of it all. And the caregivers, whether family members or professionals, should also be supported, in order to do their job in the most effective way.

Whether it was fear or lack of knowledge that made this director say what she said, the effect was still devastating. Maybe she was afraid that my son would be "a handful" and wouldn't have the resources to handle presumed behavioral issues. I say "presumed" because up to this point she had never met my kid and never asked me how what supports he needed. Regardless of the reason, we felt rejected.

SO, I decided to bring my own chair to the table. I called the director to address her concerns, and after that, my son was accepted into the program and had a wonderful two years there.

When you bring your own chair to the table, you cultivate understanding, establish meaningful connections, and build partnerships for success. In my eight years of experience working in the disability field, I have come to believe that bringing our own chairs to the table is the best way to successfully advocate for our children and families.

Let's look at the steps of this approach to give you a better picture of what I mean by bringing your own chair to the table.

1. EXPOSURE

People are afraid of the unknown. Often, when we're rejected or not included, it's because people don't know what to expect and that creates some type of fear. We all have heard of the popular saying, "you don't know what you don't know." By practicing healthy exposure, we introduced ourselves to the world.

If you want to cultivate inclusion in your church, your business, or your neighborhood, start by showing who you are to people from different cultures. If you are a minority in the midst, introduces your culture to the mainstream. Don't always wait for people to invite you, be the one to invite. I do this a lot with my family. Whether it's the local YMCA, the community center, the festival in our town, or traveling to different towns and states (and soon countries), I expose myself and my kids to different people and things.

There's a flip side to this coin. My kids and I all have conditions that could described as a special need or disability, and as we expose ourselves to the community and to the different cultures, we are also helping others learn more about us. In a sense, we help others see that there's more to us than our diagnosis.

2. UNDERSTANDING

The more you spend time with people, the more you get to know them. The more you get to know them, the better you understand them. And the more you practice exposure as mentioned above, the more you understand others and the more others understand you, and your conditions, if applicable. My friends from church I've learned so much about African culture, single parenting, disability world by me exposing myself and my kids to their world.

If you want to help people know more about the things that matter to you or the things that make you different, take time to get to know them. Don't wait for an invitation. Check online and on community bulletin boards to see what's going on around you or around the issues that matter to you, and participate.

3. CONNECTION

Exposure naturally brings understanding as understanding naturally brings connection. When people understand who you are and what you stand for, as well as why, they start to relate and you build a bond. The people that we often feel the most connected to are often the ones we've been exposed to and that we understand and accept.

For example, the way I break stigma associated with mental health is by sharing what I do and building understanding, which teaches people about mental health. I don't focus on the downside of mental health as much; society and the media do a good job of that already.

Instead, I show people that no matter how mental health has impacted them, there is hope and a life to be lived. In doing so, those affected by mental health challenges see that they can rise above the circumstances and those who take a more reserved or conservative approach toward those affected by mental health challenges learn to understand and accept them. In a sense, we all connect and bond around those challenges because we have all been affected by them either personally or through someone we know.

4. PARTNERSHIP

As we connect to others, we build partnerships for success. We no longer focus on the things that make us different or the things that we disagree on, but the connection that is built generates a bond. This bond when cultivated adequately, can help us create partnerships for success. When we feel connected, we feel supported and that support can be used to bring about change around those issues that matter to us. The people who have been exposed to you , who now understand you and what matters to you, and who you now feel connected to, can help you in your advocacy efforts.

I've spoken on panels at state-wide trainings and workshops to help Support Coordinators and other professionals become more inclusive. I have also spoken at multiple mental health conferences to share hope and wellness strategies for the same reasons mentioned above. Additionally, I build partnerships with organizations, associations, and foundations that support the causes I care about and that has expanded my support and it has given me more tools for advocacy. I'm often a minority at those tables, but I have learned that bringing my own chair to the table helps all of us. It can be intimidating to join those tables, but it benefits more people than I could ever imagine and for that reason, it's a risk worth taking.

Chou lives in Harrisburg, Pennsylvania, where she offers person-centered counseling and consultation to persons living with disabilities and their caregivers. She has a Masters Degree in Human Services from Liberty University. She attends West Shore Brethren in Christ of Mechanicsburg, PA.

Social Media sites:
https://linkedin.com/in/chouhallegra/
www.graceandhopeconsulting.com
www.facebook.com/graceandhopeconsulting
https://twitter.com/GHConsultingLLC
https://www.instagram.com/graceandhopeconsultingllc/
https://www.youtube.com/channel/UC3pRF8PUoYL8KFg-flSx2W6g/videos
https://plus.google.com/118300558327763459329
https://anchor.fm/grace-hope-consulting

LEARNING TO EMERGE
ELIZABETH SCHROEDER

The first time I thought about running for public office was in March 2017. I was in the passenger seat of my husband's car as we drove through a perennial field of colorful candidate yard signs. Both being unapologetic political junkies, we were chatting about the upcoming spring election, just a couple of short weeks away.

"Do you see me running for office someday?" I blurted out, surprising myself. I had no idea where the question had come from. It wasn't something I had ever given any conscious thought, though it makes sense in hindsight. Still reeling from election night 2016, I had spent the past few months feeling increasingly listless and desperate to do something, never quite sure what that something was.

My husband didn't seem at all caught off guard by the question. "Yes," he said conclusively, almost as though he had been waiting for me to ask. "Definitely."

He has to say that, I reminded myself, and pushed the notion out of my mind.

The second time I thought about running for office was more than a year later, when I learned that my Alder was stepping down from Madison, Wisconsin's Common Council.

Maybe I could run, I thought, and was immediately hit with an overwhelming sense of panic. The idea felt exhilarating, but also paralyzingly scary, like a dirty secret I was terrified of letting slip. My mind buzzed with questions I didn't know how to answer. Did I have enough experience? Not really. Did it matter? Maybe. Was I smart enough? I thought so. Could I, a textbook introvert and hopeless networker, convincingly sell myself as an elected official? Doubtful. What if I ran and lost? *What if I won?*

Even if I could convince myself that this was a good idea, there was one enormous, obvious hurdle: I had absolutely no idea what I was doing. This is clearly evidenced by the Word document I started that day and recently revisited. The document has four columns: pros, cons, to-do's, and the longest one, questions.

- What forms do I need to file? With whom? When?
- Do I need a campaign manager?
- How much money do I need to raise?

At some point, desperate for information and with no idea who to ask, I opened a new search window and typed "how to run for local office in Wisconsin." I'm not sure exactly what I was looking for, but the thing I needed fell right into my lap: Emerge Wisconsin.

Emerge is a six-month-long training program that recruits and prepares Democratic women to run for all levels of elected office, from city council and school board all the way to the U.S. Senate. Their mission is to change the face of politics, breaking down the systemic barriers that women face when running for office, and bringing missing and much-needed voices to the table.

Each year, Emerge Wisconsin selects about 25 women from across the state to receive training on topics like public speaking, political fundraising, networking, and campaign strategy. I knew right away that this was my starting point. A few weeks after stumbling across their website, I submitted my application materials for the class of 2019. I interviewed a month later.

Shortly before Christmas 2018, I was accepted into the program.

I began my time with Emerge expecting to learn and grow, and I did. I learned all the answers to my long list of questions, plus many more I hadn't even known to ask. What I didn't expect was to be profoundly changed by my experience. The biggest and most important lessons I learned had very little to do with politics, and a whole lot to do with who I was and who I had the potential to be.

First and foremost, I learned that **self-confidence is a public service**. When I first learned that I had been accepted into Emerge Wisconsin's 2019 class and began reading through my classmates' bios and resumes, I was positive there had been a mistake. These women were educated, engaged, and successful. There were veterans, professors, nonprofit leaders, entrepreneurs, and community activists. Some were already serving in elected or appointed office. How could I ever have thought I belonged in that group? Who was I to take a spot from someone more deserving? A few months into the program, I confessed these feelings to a classmate who I admired and respected deeply. "I felt exactly the same way," she told me. I was astonished. If this badass woman was harboring the same self-doubt that I was, then what the hell were we all doing? Why were we wasting time questioning our own worth instead of owning it and manifesting it into the change we were all clearly capable of creating? When you've been socialized since birth to diminish your own accomplishments and shrink yourself for the comfort of others, metaphorically standing up and declaring "I deserve to be here" feels somehow vulgar or uncouth. It's not. In fact, it's necessary. As long as women are kept feeling small, seeing ourselves as unworthy, our critical perspectives and voices will remain unheard. Our communities need us to see ourselves as leaders.

I learned that magic happens when women help each other. We've all heard–and most of us have internalized–the harmful, misogynistic tropes about groups of women. They're petty; they're nothing but drama; all they do is gossip behind each other's backs. The truth is that there is no support system stronger than a group of like-minded, empowered women. Since meeting my Emerge cohort in January 2019, I've come to lean on them in a way that's powerful and unique. It's a relationship unlike any other in my life. Emerge uses the word "sisterhood" for a reason. Though many of us are separated by distance or busy schedules or general life craziness, there is absolutely no doubt that my Emerge sisters are my people. We've seen each other shine, face fears, fail, and be vulnerable. We lift each other up and cheer each other on. When you're a woman trying to carve out a place in a world long dominated by men, there's something incredibly nourishing about having a group of women that you can turn to and say "I need to vent" or "I need help" or even "I need a pep talk." Since starting Emerge, I've made a concerted effort to be part of that support system for every woman in my life. We need each other, now more than ever.

Finally, I learned that **elected officials are people, too**. Yes, this sounds painfully obvious, which it is. It was also the hardest lesson for me to learn. I can't say exactly when this realization hit me. The first time I was introduced to a state legislator, I felt like I was meeting a celebrity. As someone who spent most of my childhood and young adulthood trying to please teachers, coaches, and bosses, my instinct was to be meek and deferential. After all, this was a *politician*. By our graduation weekend, which took place at the Wisconsin Democratic Convention, I was walking up and saying "hi" to lawmakers that I knew personally. I was talking to my friends about their eventual runs for Wisconsin's state legislature and even Congress. An interesting shift happens when you start to see elected officials less as untouchable authority figures and more as everyday people with cool jobs; it becomes exponentially easier to picture yourself among them. Those who hold elected office aren't necessarily smarter, wealthier, or more educated than the rest of us. They are citizens who care about their communities, saw an opportunity to serve, and had the guts to go for it. If they can do it, I can do it. And if I can do it, so can you.

I still have not run for office. It's possible I never will. The difference is that I now know I can, if and when I choose to. I've joined a lineup of incredible, qualified women who are ready and willing to jump up and serve when our communities need us. And when we do, we'll be backed by a national network of sisters who want nothing more than to see us succeed.

Emerge currently has programs in 29 states, and is actively growing. If you believe in equal representation at all levels of government and empowering women to succeed, I urge you to consider supporting Emerge America or your state affiliate. And if you, like me, have ever felt even the tiniest, quietest calling toward public service, I can't recommend Emerge highly enough. Run or not, win or lose, you'll come out of it a better, bolder person.

Elizabeth Schroeder is the digital director at NextGen Wisconsin, as well as a mother of two. In addition to her role at NextGen, she serves on the Madison, Wisconsin's Early Childhood Care and Education Committee. She is a 2019 graduate of Emerge Wisconsin.

PART II:
HOW DO YOU GET INVOLVED?

This section is all about different ways to get involved in your community or in a policy change or political process. Just like there is no one reason for getting involved, there is no one way to be involved. In the essays that follow, our writers describe the many avenues of social action, ranging from activities that take you out of your neighborhood, and sometimes your comfort zone, to simple but meaningful actions to take right in your own home. As Jennifer Rosen Heinz describes in her essay, your personality and your skills can be taken into consideration when deciding how to get involved. Whether you're a working mother with full schedule or a stay-at-home mom with a new baby, there's a place for you.

If you take anything away from this section, our hope is that you'll understand that you are wanted and needed. Your voice is powerful, your actions, big or small, will move mountains.

POLITICAL ENGAGEMENT: WE NEED YOU
JENNIFER ROSEN HEINZ

Politics is messy. Democracy is messy. Finding consensus and solving problems is messy. Just because something is messy, it doesn't mean it's not worth doing!

No career is more reviled or maligned than that of the politician. Yet when it comes to decisions that can have huge effects on our lives and our world, politicians have some of the greatest impact. It's easy to criticize the process from afar (actually, and from up close, too), but it's important to keep in mind that especially now, more and more people are jumping into politics who never would have even considered it before. And that's great! The more diverse the make-up of our elected officials, the more likelihood that we can have a democracy that represents all of us.

The great thing about getting involved in politics is that there are LOTS of ways to do it, and you very likely can find a way to work for a cause, a party, or a candidate that you believe in. One of the first questions I always ask people is what do you like to do?

- Are you a person who loves to train other people?

- Are you a worker bee?
- Do you have mad graphic design skills?
- Do you like planning and executing events?
- Would you rather be a behind-the-scenes bean counter kind of person?
- Would you prefer to not volunteer, but throw money at the issue?

All of these roles (and more) are really important things that candidates and campaigns need to produce and manage. You may be the missing piece they're looking for!

Here are some of the many ways to get involved. You can do one, you can do many. But the most important thing is that you do something, no matter how small or big. Paraphrasing Dr. Seuss, nothing will change unless someone like you cares an awful lot.

VOLUNTEER

Volunteers are the bread and butter of every campaign. They are the ones who do the things that you realistically can't pay people to do. The small stuff that makes the difference in getting the message out there about a campaign issue or candidate.

Lots of people wonder: with the advent of the internet, does this stuff really matter? I am here to tell you, YES. It does matter, and it can win or lose elections.

If you already have an issue or candidate that you would like to support, the best way to get involved is to call or get in touch with their local campaign office. For more issues-related groups, find out where and when the next meeting is. Get on their email list. Find their Facebook page. Set yourself a goal of getting in the door. I can't stress this enough.

IF YOU DO NOT WALK IN THE DOOR, YOU WILL NOT GET INVOLVED.

That's because we are all creatures of habit with busy lives and entire libraries full of excuses. Stop listening to the excuses. Your ONLY job is to show up. Everything else springs from that. Showing up is the hardest part.

Once you show up, the next goal is to make a new acquaintance, and to sign up for something. Right there on the spot. Or if there's nothing to sign up for, go and talk to someone who is in charge and ask them what needs to be done; or tell them what you'd especially like to do to help.

There are thousands of people who wanted to get involved with an issue, but can't or won't show up. And for those who do show up, it's important to note that you immediately double the campaign's capacity to do something. If the campaign had only one person who could update events on our Facebook page and they gain another, they can do DOUBLE the amount of work, in half of the time. When you are talking about organizations that run on little to no money, that's a huge gain.

Most volunteers on political campaigns will do one (or many) of these activities:

Canvassing - Also called "door knocking," canvassing is going door to door in a specific geographic area to talk to potential voters and leave pamphlets or literature about the issue or candidate. Generally, these days you will canvass or door knock only at specific or targeted addresses of likely friendly voters, which are provided to you by the campaign. You can do this alone or with a partner (my fave).

Phone Banking - If the campaign has an office, you may go down to the office during specific times to do phone banking from the campaign's office and phones. Some campaigns run virtual phone banks where you don't even have to leave your house! You are provided with a call list and a script, and the rest is just dialing and talking. Everyone is nervous at first, but you'll hit your groove in no time. Conversations are so important in motivating people to get out for a candidate.

Text Banking - Don't like talking to other humans? Many other humans don't either! We're more and more used to only taking calls from numbers that we recognize. That's where text banking comes in. There are great smartphone apps and internet-based programs that can allow campaign volunteers to send out texts to many people at once. But they need someone to set it in motion, and to field responses and questions. It's so easy, even someone who isn't tech savvy can catch on quickly.

Organizing - This is a broad term used to describe the activities of people who work to get volunteers for the campaign, to put them where they need to be, and to strategize about how to best use campaign resources to reach the most voters. This can be a really fun job because you will have contact with many different people, and see the results of people working together for a common cause. Organizers may be volunteers or, as in presidential campaigns, may be paid campaign staff.

Lit Drops, Candy, Envelope stuffing, Outreach, oh my!

- In other words—the miscellaneous grab bag of things that make campaigns work. Maybe they need someone to pick up brochures from the printer and deliver them to the volunteer who will coordinate distribution. Maybe you have a bunch of Halloween candy left over, and you want to drop it off to fuel the campaign volunteers. (Donuts, coffee, and catering trays are usually a very welcome sight, too!) Maybe envelopes need to be stuffed. Maybe they need someone on behalf of the campaign to go staff a table at a community event.

Whatever you do—whether it's small or big, whether it's something you're new to or old hand at—campaigns can and do need you, your presence, and your talents—to make a difference.

USING YOUR VOICE

Now, more than ever, we have so many different ways that we can use our voices to bring attention to issues and people who need attention. Some of them are as old as time, and some are new opportunities, but they all are ways to reach people, motivate them, and to draw awareness.

Letter to the Editor - While some people still receive their local paper in physical format, many people have changed to reading their paper online. Which means that the Letter to the Editor has not yet gone the way of the Dodo. Letters to the editor are usually 200-300 words (check with the particular publication for their guidelines before writing) and in electronic form, they're great to share on Facebook pages and in groups.

Writing or Calling your representatives - First rule of

thumb is do not waste your time signing online petitions to your representatives. They do not pay attention to them. They do, however, count and pay attention to direct calls to their offices on particular topics, as well as good old physical letters. Email is also categorized, but often not read, but rather scanned for particular keywords.

As with all communication, make sure to let the office or legislator know if you're a constituent and give them your address and zip code. For issues that need immediate attention, calling is always best. For longer-term issues, mail is fine, though expect at least a month's delay from the time you send your letter to any possible response of their office, since many politicians have their mail scanned and secured before it is even delivered to their offices.

Remember to be polite and concise when you speak with anyone in a legislator's office. The people answering the phones are often low-level interns, and as you can imagine, speaking with angry people all day is probably its own special hell. I often try and write down the name of the person with whom I've spoken and remind them if I've spoken with them before. It builds a little more of a personal connection.

Community Forums - Not all public officials will hold town halls or the like, but if they do, plan to show up. Ask a question. Kindly and politely put them on the spot. Ask their advice in how you can best advocate for a certain issue or position. Or take them to task for an inconsistency or falsehood. SHOW UP. I can guarantee you that even if you're nervous, they're more afraid of being held accountable to you... as they should be!

SOCIAL MEDIA

Social media can be a great tool for spreading awareness of an issue, and motivating people to act. It can also be extremely annoying. The key is seeing social media as a tool, just like other tools in your toolbox. Think about what you share, and how you frame it. Are you offering new information? Are you giving someone an action they can take?

Think before you share. If it isn't productive, or if it's the same meme people have seen 1000 times, don't share it. Social media isn't only about your self-expression; it's also about your audience. If you have lots of friends who may disagree with you on an issue, look for ways to present an issue that will sway them, knowing their background, their priorities, and their values.

Invite people to join you for specific actions—a letter-writing campaign, a protest. Ask them to call their representative on a certain issue, and leave you a comment that says DONE, or a gif. Try and make it fun. I often will challenge my friends to do something, and report that they've done it, and then will enter them into a drawing for a cup of coffee (usually in the form of a $5 gift card to their favorite coffee shop). Everyone loves coffee.

DONATE

Money in politics. It's the elephant in the room.

In the United States of America, we have an electoral system which has specifically been designed to allow individuals, corporations, unions, and outside interest groups to contribute money to issues and candidates. Do I love it? Honestly, no. I personally do not believe that money should equal speech—the more money you have, the more say you have in how you are represented.

In fact, I would argue that most people don't like it. Or they like the idea of having more say, but don't like the fact that others can buy that privilege, too.

After having talked with many politicians, I can tell you honestly that many of them do not like the pressure to raise exorbitant amounts of cash just to be considered a serious contender—even in a primary election. Even in small, local races where the actual political position is part-time, and makes no money. Sure, there are others who would like to use politics as a way to make money (and lots of it). But for just as many people, they would rather not have to spend their time "dialing for dollars."

Yet, until the point at which we can elect enough legislators who want to get money back OUT of politics, this trend will continue. And to my mind, holding candidates to a standard which requires them to eschew the current norm of fundraising is tying them to a strategy which largely fails, given the current paradigm. It also unnecessarily burdens candidates who are women, LGBTQ+, or people of color (POC), who statistically don't have access to the same networks of wealth that straight white men do.

So, that's why it's important to support and CONTRIBUTE to politicians who take a pledge to try and get money out of politics—especially from underrepresented groups. Then, hold them to their promises. If they don't deliver on them after being elected, ask them about it. Hold them accountable. Pressure more candidates to do something to change the current system.

Plus, you might get a nifty t-shirt or bumper sticker. You might get a thank you call, or be invited to a private event where you can talk to the candidate about an issue that is important to you. Then, tell your friends about it. Post a picture of you with the candidate, and tell them why you are supporting them. Challenge others to give as well. Have a little house party where everyone brings a favorite dish from around the world, and you supply beverages. Ask for donations. Double, triple, quadruple your impact by inspiring others to put their money where their mouths are.

RUN

Women, on average, must be ASKED 20+ times whether they will run for office before they seriously consider it. Hold yourself with the confidence of a man. WHY NOT YOU?

If you're considering what a run for political office might look like, and how to test the waters, there are organizations out there who have been effective in training candidates for office, and helping them to decide what to run for. From local school board to statewide office, to the national stage, it's important to know the basics of how to run an effective campaign.

She Should Run is a non-partisan group that helps women get elected to office.

Emerge America prepares women who identify as Democrats to run for office.

Higher Heights encourages and supports women of color to run for office.

Many of the women who take part in programs run by these organizations not only run for office, but win. They form mutually supportive networks of women who help mentor each other and continue to bring women into every layer of government.

The truth is that whether you consider politics something you've always had an interest in, or whether you are just now considering running for office, it is paramount to the future of our society that we have more women in positions of power. As Shirley Chisholm, the first African American woman elected to congress, famously said, "If they don't give you a seat at the table, bring a folding chair." Do not wait for someone to find you, to ask you. Decide what's important to you and demand a seat at the table.

HATE PARTISAN POLITICS?

Though I really hope that through this discussion, you've found something that suits your talents and your interests, it's ok if running for office or helping someone run for office isn't for you. There are lots of other things you can do to advocate for the causes that mean the most to you.

Voter Suppression - Given the recurrence of so much voter suppression, one of the areas in greatest need of attention is challenging things like voter ID laws, which make it much more difficult for poor people to vote. (Any time you add steps or hurdles to voting, voter participation suffers. Voter ID laws are engineered to take advantage of this and suppress turnout).

Register people to vote - Many states allow online voter registration, or even in-person, day-of election registration. However, the greatest indicator that people WILL vote is that they are registered. Call your local elections office and ask how to become deputized to help register people to vote. Contact the League of Women Voters and ask them how you can help increase awareness and turnout for elections.

Advocate for an end to gerrymandering - (the process of drawing voting district maps to illegally sway elections.) Some states like North Carolina, Pennsylvania, and Wisconsin have recently had challenges to the partisan way that their voting maps were configured, which often disadvantaged Democrats and minorities. Join the ACLU and fund the fight to challenge and re-draw partisan maps.

Work the polls - Contact your local election commission and get trained to be a poll worker. Learn the ins-and-outs and legalities of helping to make sure that every vote counts and that our elections are fair and follow the laws.

Drive people to the polls - Transportation can be a real barrier for some voters—especially those with disabilities, those who do not own their own vehicles or are not close to public transportation. Anything you can do to make it easier for people to exercise their right to vote is a patriotic and noble thing to do.

Vote. Early. - If your state or city has the option of casting an early vote or voting early by absentee ballot, consider doing it. You never know what might come up on the actual day of the election, and that way you know your vote will be cast and counted. Also, this frees you up to volunteer on election day.

Raise Awareness - One of the most important things you can do without "taking a side" is sharing information with others on upcoming elections. When is election day? What is at stake? What are the barriers to voting that people should know about and plan ahead for?

Choose an issue - Get involved with an organization that advocates on behalf of one particular issue.

Care about reducing gun violence and stopping mass shootings? Join Moms Demand Action for Gun Sense in America.

Worried about the environment? Join Sierra Club.

Show up to government hearings about issues that are important to you. People who show up and let their voices be heard make a difference. In fact, they make a 100% difference over those who sit on the couch and don't do anything.

It may sound trite, but I often think about the fact that being involved in the political process is, for me, kind of like going to the gym. The hardest part is getting motivated to do something. But once I'm there, I'm always glad I went. And even when I do things that are outside of my comfort zone, even things that I find difficult, I almost always find them rewarding afterwards. I know I am contributing to creating a world that I want to see my children thrive in. And I know that that world will not come about with my—and your—engagement, energy, and showing up.

Jennifer Rosen Heinz is the founder and editor in chief of Use Your OUTSIDE VOICE-www.facebook.com/outsidevoicesunited - A media outlet which keeps people informed and motivated in a world where sometimes the news makes us feel helpless. 50%

of the profits from OUTSIDE VOICE go directly to getting women of Color elected to public office. She is the co-creator of the Kindness is Everything sign, which raised over $200k for the ACLU and other nonprofits. She is also a volunteer leader for Moms Demand Action for Gun Sense in America and often does public speaking to encourage others to find their activist passions.

FROM FRUSTRATED-AS-HELL TO GETTING-SHIT-DONE: ONE MOM'S ADVICE ON CHOOSING YOUR CAUSE AND BECOMING AN ACTIVIST

SHANTI BRIEN

Last Saturday I returned to my hometown—not for a high school reunion or pool-side relaxation with a Danielle Steele novel as was my teenage tradition—but with the intent to win back the House of Representatives. The oven-like heat of noon in mid-July reminded me of why I left there. Modesto, famous as the birthplace of cruising and the capital of cheap wine, is also hotter than hell in the summer. And now it's the epicenter of the movement to win back the House of Representatives in November.

I arrived in Modesto at the encouragement of my best college friend, Susie. She emailed me after news of the impending Supreme Court disaster hit the news. "What are we going to do!?!" she asked. For months, I had wallowed in overwhelm and fatigue. I watched too many horrible, unimaginable events happen at the same time: children ripped from their parents and held for indefinite periods in jail-like conditions, the constant de-legitimization of the investigation into Russia's influence on our elections, and now the likely appointment of an ultra-conservative Supreme Court Justice resulting in the end to reproductive rights as we know them and the beginning of an age of hyper gun ownership. Susie's email woke me up a bit and luckily, she knew what we were going to do. We would take a girls-only, political action, ass-kicking road trip!

More than 100 people met at the park in Modesto to get trained on canvassing, pick up buttons and fliers, and receive a list of assignments. We would be pounding the pavement for a young, smart Democrat trying to out-seat a long-term incumbent Republican. Susie and I were assigned a mostly-immigrant neighborhood because Susie speaks Spanish like a native and I can bumble along saying "hace calor!" On our way across town we used Google Translate to help us with "Congress," "candidate," "health care," and other obscure political vocabulary. We lathered up in sunscreen, donned our political pins, stickers and clip board and set off!

We met a family outside hosting a garage sale in the baking heat. One 19-year girl had registered to vote at school. After talking with us, she committed to vote for our candidate and registered to vote by mail, one of our most important goals of the day. Her mom initially expressed uncertainty about the candidates, but after learning about our candidate, especially his stance on expanding health care and helping immigrants, she was all in. We registered a sister and a cousin to vote, too! All of that in one stop. Plus, we chatted in Spanish and refilled on water. After about twenty more houses and a success rate of close to 50%, we hit the taco truck and the convenience store for Super Big Gulp-sized iced tea and cheap packaged cookies. Despite my unhealthy food choices, I consider the day a success. I met generous, friendly people, caught up with my best friend and hopefully did a small part in flipping the House. I think I'll bring my teenagers next time. They are persistent, hearty and "woke." And they love tacos!

So the question is, how does a busy mom move from overwhelmed and weary to focused and motivated? From frustrated-as-hell to getting-shit-done?

These are my recommendations:

1. Focus on what's most compelling or easiest.

The overwhelm is real. I'm a working mom with three kids, two in club sports, all in braces, with an extra part-time teaching job, a husband that travels, and a desire to make homemade, organic meals. But I know how to deal with it. Just like moms prioritize one kid's needs when they hit crisis mode, activists must prioritize and focus. Consider: of all of the issues you care about, which pulls on you the most? Which keeps you up at night? Which do you have a specific skill or special interest in? If you still can't narrow the field, just do what is easiest. A friend invites you to a political discussion or a fundraiser for a candidate? So easy, no research needed and she'll likely serve wine. In the past, I focused on the Women's March and giving to Planned Parenthood. With two teenage daughters who were huge Hillary supporters, those seemed the most compelling. Now, I am prioritizing the mid-term elections and supporting House candidates that have a decent chance of winning. I'm even more focused on California House candidates because they are closest to me, easiest to get to and I can sway friends and family to help them too.

2. Find a buddy.

Despite the pull of cheap wine, I would not have gone to Modesto without a buddy. Susie and I had travelled to Nevada for the 2016 presidential elections together, too. We acted as poll monitors on the election days and generally helped around Hillary's headquarters in Northern Nevada. In our trips to Reno and Modesto, Susie and I had plenty of driving time to catch up, talk about our kids' looming high school years, creative dinners for our growing brood of children, and of course, politics.

I also have a loose-knit group of friends who invite each other to political talks, fundraisers and marches. We all have teenagers and when their friends get involved, my teenagers are much more likely to join. Finally, I'm part of a group in my little town of Piedmont which gathers our collective knowledge and resources to locate organizations doing good work and invite rising leaders to come talk to us about issues. As a smart woman once said, "It takes a village."

3. Take baby steps.

Like any new habit, becoming an activist will more likely happen if you start small. I've started a mindfulness practice (to beat the weariness and the overwhelm) and I only do two minutes each morning. Even though I could do more, I want the practice to be consistent and long-term. Same with activism.

Many people burned out right after the 2016 elections. But if the last two years have taught us anything, it's that we need consistent, long-term, and dedicated civic involvement. So here are my ideas for baby steps: register to vote, register to vote by mail which is even easier (see suggestion #2), mail in the ballot the day it comes, give $5 or $10 to the congressional race nearest to you, put a sign in your front yard, send a super-short email to your congressmember telling them what is important to you (find their email address here: https://www.house.gov/representatives/find-your-representative), consider sending an email quarterly, calendaring it a year in advance and setting a reminder.

4. Involve the kiddos.

This is the key for busy moms. Not everyone has the time or money to hire a babysitter to go and canvass around town for a local candidate. You can bring your kids to marches. My kids loved making signs for the Women's March in Oakland. You can bring your kids with you to the polling place (if you decide not to vote by mail). You can bring your kids with you to the grocery store while you buy nourishing snacks and hydration for the people out canvassing. One friend involved her pre-teen in making phone calls for a get-out-the-vote drive. You can do something as simple as talking to your kids about political ads when they pop up on TV or stuff your mail box to the point of explosion. As moms, we have the opportunity to teach our children about taking action, becoming engaged community members, and standing up for what's right. We each have the opportunity to become involved—even in the smallest ways—

with causes we care about, in order to make large-scale change.

So onward, activist moms! Let's go get some shit done.

Shanti is a recovering NFL wife, a lawyer-to-criminals and a mother of three. She writes about family and social justice issues including her cowboy and Indian family, Colin Kaepernick, and raising teenage girls. She is the Co-Founder of Daylight Justice which provides educational experiences about fairness and inclusion for criminal justice professionals and civic leaders. https://medium.com/@shantibrightbrien

BE THE VOICE
CHOU HELLEGRA

In a society where people are afraid of what is different, be the voice. When others only stand with what they know, be the voice.

When you see others being secluded, segregated, bullied, be the voice.

Be the voice that stands up for what is right.

Be the voice that stands for justice.

Be the voice that calls out inequality.

Be the voice that teaches others that we were all born equal and that we all belong.

Be the voice that reminds others that all human life should be valued, that we are all worthy of love and acceptance, just the way we are.

My name is Chou Hallegra and I am a woman of many abilities and challenges and a mother of three children with diverse abilities and challenges as well. I've also had the privilege and honor to work with people that society has labeled as disabled, special needs, and/or handicapped. I am also a black woman. I am originally from Brazzaville, Congo (Africa). Hence, I fit both the "disabled" label as well as the "minority label."

In my diverse roles as an individual of these communities, a caregiver to my children, a consultant and ally to the people I support through my work, there is one thing that I aim to do every single day. It's to be the voice. I want to be the voice that reminds all of us that we are the people. And no matter our labels, no matter our diagnoses, no matter our differences, we are all people and we need each other.

If like me, you too want to be the voice, here are 3 simple (but not necessarily easy) ways to get started:

1. Be intentional about inclusion

Do not wait for the cultural days at school or at your local community center. Although these events are good ways to meet people from other cultures and abilities, real connections happen when we are intentional about building relationships with others who are different from us.

Invite that Russian neighbor over for tea or knock on the Nigerian neighbor's door and introduce yourself. Instead of simply following an Indian dancer on social media, go have lunch with your Indian coworker. Visit your child's school and invite the kid in the wheelchair to your home for a playdate.

It's time we start cultivating real inclusive communities and it begins with you.

Don't just wait to be invited—invite.

Don't wait to be explained to—ask. Instead of running away from what is different from us, be it differences in race or ability, let's embrace it. Run towards what it is that you are afraid of. The closer you get, the more you realize we are all the same. We do have more in common than not.

2. Educate yourself, then educate others

The more we hang out with people different from us, the more we learn about them and those differences. Yet, the more educated we are, the more accepting we become.

Read books about other cultures. Watch videos about disabilities. Attend conferences on topics so foreign to your world that you feel like an outsider. We often invest our time and intellect in things that we value. If you want to value people from different races and people with disabilities, then start learning more about the people from those groups.

The more you learn about them, the more you will have to talk about when you actually meet one of them. Then you won't feel like an outsider anymore but rather as one of them. And I guarantee you that you will find many of us who love to teach others about our cultures and abilities. Then the more you learn, the more you can educate others as well.

3. Be a role model

Your kids are watching, so are your nephews, nieces, siblings and other relatives. We all know that actions speak louder than words, so you can't tell them to be accepting of others if they have never seen you practice that.

Don't just be a talker, be a doer. In other words, don't just talk the talk but actually walk the walk. Don't just read great resources and tell others about what you read, but instead show them what you learned. If we want change, we need to be the change.

Although these three tips don't seem like much, you'll find that they can be difficult to accomplish because of the ways we have been conditioned by society. As you become more intentional about promoting inclusion and get up close and personal with folks different from you, it will feel uncomfortable at first. But whoever accomplished much by being comfortable? No one!

I encourage you to stretch yourself to be an inclusive person. No matter your upbringing or how far you've distanced yourself from others who are not like you, you can choose today to embrace diversity. You can stop doing what everyone else in your family or community did. You can choose to live differently and to raise your children differently. We are all beautiful pieces of this mosaic we call World, it's time we start valuing each other as such.

To you, my white friend, reading this, I say "be the voice".

To you, my black friend, reading this, I say "be the voice".

To you, my friend, who communicates verbally, I say, "Be the voice".

To you, my friend, who communicates with the use of signs, gestures, and technology, I say, "Be the voice".

To you, my friend, who ambulates with your legs and feet, I say, "Be the voice".

To you, my friend, who ambulates with a cane, walker, or chair, I say, "Be the voice".

To all my friends of different abilities and experiences, I say, "Be the voice".

A child can be the voice just as an adult can.

A woman can be the voice just as a man can.

A single mom can be the voice just as a married woman can.

A person with a disability can be the voice just as someone without a disability can.

I choose to be the voice. Will you?

Chou Hallegra is the Founder of Grace & Hope Consulting, LLC. As a Mental Health Counselor, "Ability" Consultant and Christian Life Coach, she is passionate about helping women and children achieve emotional wellness, reach their full potential and live fulfilling lives. Chou enjoys connecting with people from diverse backgrounds and ethnicities and is involved with many advocacy organizations. Chou and her family live in Pennsylvania.

Social Media sites:
https://linkedin.com/in/chouhallegra/
www.graceandhopeconsulting.com
www.facebook.com/graceandhopeconsulting
https://twitter.com/GHConsultingLLC
https://www.instagram.com/graceandhopeconsultingllc/
https://www.youtube.com/channel/UC3pRF8PUoYL8KFg-fISx2W6g/videos
https://plus.google.com/118300558327763459329
https://anchor.fm/grace-hope-consulting

THE WIZARD OF OZ: DOROTHY AS A SOCIAL ACTIVIST
MARY WHEATLEY

We're all familiar with the story of *The Wizard of OZ*. An old classic that to this day makes me want to pull a blanket over my head when the witch comes sweeping down on her broom. The story begins with the main character, Dorothy, being carried up by a fierce tornado and dropped into a magical, yet unfamiliar land. She is determined at all costs, to get back to the loving arms of her family; and thus, begins her journey.

In so many ways, Dorothy represents moms who seek change in the world around them but are uncertain how to move the substantial mountains in the way. Many moms sit on untapped reserves of energy, intelligence, motivation, and determination to change social and political ills, despite their awareness of needed change. Perhaps it is the fear of the wicked witch and not wanting to face the fierce winds of opposition. Possibly, there is no yellow brick road to follow.

As Dorothy set about her journey to find her way home, she encountered many challenges. Along the way, she met and engaged new allies for her plight. She would discover that each had their own desires for change and they teamed up to take on the challenges together. They embraced the journey even though they were met with fierce opposition. Never did Dorothy or her friends give up; their desire to change their situation was greater than the enormity of the task to accomplish it.

Dorothy and her friends had overcome many trials and tests but, in the end, she conquered her oppressor with a simple bucket of water. It was through Dorothy's desire to love and protect her friend, the scarecrow, (who had been set ablaze by the wicked witch), that she ultimately wins the day. Dorothy won the coveted witches' broom, not with violence but with her loving commitment to another. Ultimately, she destroys the witch and saves the land of OZ from its unwanted oppressor.

As the film concludes, we see each of the characters receive accolades for their bravery and perseverance. But Dorothy, the leader of the pack finds that the aid of the great and powerful "wizard" would elude her as he floats off in his hot air balloon before Dorothy could climb on board. Lo and behold, in true Dorothy fashion, Glinda The Good Witch comes to her aid and offers Dorothy a reminder of her own inner power. Dorothy would find her way back home, not by the aid of the great and powerful "wizard" but entirely through her own means. She ultimately achieves her desired return home when she realizes that everything she needs was inside her this whole time. Through her challenging journey, Dorothy needed to experience her own power, in order to come around to using it.

Moms, you possess all that you need to make the political and social changes you desire. Tap into your inner strengths, find your team and put your trust in those who will support your journey, despite the obstacles. With a unified front, you will see your way to the change you seek.

FIND YOUR CAUSE

Be your own advocate; learn to speak up for yourself about the rights and options that are important to you.

Familiarize yourself about the cause you are seeking to change. Why was the rule/policy/course of action initiated? How would you like to see it amended?

Find your tribe; don't be shy about talking to others about your ideas. Start a petition, form a group of those interested in the same changes you desire.

Trust your tribe; gather support and confidence aligning yourself with a like-minded community.

Follow the required Course of Action; present a proposal, speak with the policy makers, administrators, or auxiliary staff to get your concern on the agenda. Follow the procedure required to get your grievance/s heard.

Carry on with perseverance; be persistent and accept that policy changes take time. If your first attempt does not yield desired results, consider revising your proposal and don't quit. Seek to get on the following agenda and remember that solutions take compromise, be willing to let go of something for the greater gain.

Mary Wheatley, is the founder of Inspired Parent Coach. She coaches parents to rediscover their strengths as a means to shore up their own self awareness, and become the optimal parent for their children. Creative by nature, she began her "encore" career after 30 years in the design field. Mary enjoys co-creating solutions with parents, to help them overcome the immense challenges they face in today's chaotic world. She is a Graduate of Seattle Pacific University's accredited Graduate program for Parent Coaching and is a certified Parent Coach. Mary and her husband live in Hawaii; where her two now young adult daughters were born and raised. You may learn more about her services by visiting inspiredparentcoach.com

PART 3
RAISING TINY ACTIVISTS

We've talked about the "whys" we've gotten involved and the "hows" of getting involved, now let's talk about activities and actions that will bring your kids into the mix as well. Raising children who are socially aware and understand that their voice matters will result in a society that feels compelled to be part of the discussion, across all issues. It doesn't even have to be political – it can be an involvement in community and social activities that help them develop a compassion for a segment of society that they would not normally be exposed to. It's amazing the life-long impact serving food to the homeless can have on a child, or even adopting a family for Christmas. The following essays are a few ideas on how to involve your children.

RAISING WARRIORS: HOW PARENTS EVERYWHERE CAN SAVE THE WORLD ONE CHILD AT A TIME
KATIE WHITE

My children were never supposed to be activists.

I don't think most children are supposed to be activists, and certainly not by choice or design. Being an activist requires both an awareness of critical issues and a sense of accountability and commitment. It requires a willingness to commit, to take action, to reject the status quo. Most parents would not wish these things for their kids, in part because so often real activism requires solidarity with others who seek justice and, to some degree, we want to protect our children for as long as we can from the harsh realities of the world.

There are a lot of problems in the world. People suffer. The environment is on the brink of disaster. Leaders seem more concerned with reelection than with creating solutions.

Activists want to change all that and they will do whatever it takes to make it happen.

Raising kids to be activists is not for the faint of heart.

I am not a born activist. I came from an "aware family" but not an activist one. My sister, brother and I had a careful, suburban California upbringing. We discussed the issues of the day with my mother who was very open about things that mattered to her. But she wasn't very "active" in her desire to change the world. She preferred reading books to political marches. My father's idea of being a change agent was switching his political affiliation from R to D in response to the 1986 tax overhaul—he's still railing about that offense.

When I married a nice bloke from England who supposedly liked football (soccer), living most of his life outdoors (we met at summer camp), and "going down the pub" on a Friday evening for a pint of beer, I had no idea our lives were about to change. He came from a long line of builders and factory workers and his only experience of changing the political order was the miners strikes in Thatcher's England and even that wasn't enough to convince him to give up a good pub crawl in favor of political organizing.

So it comes as a bit of a shock to me as the 20 years of our marriage has gone by that we've become known as activists. My husband became a leader in Virginia environmental circles and I have become, if not an activist, then at the very least, an advocate for my work in the nonprofit sector.

We've been in some pretty incredible places and been witness to history. We marched in Edinburgh, Scotland in 2006 in order to Make Poverty History and were with the counterprotesters in Charlottesville when a car plowed into crowd killing Heather Hyer and injuring dozens more. We've fought against pipelines, rallied for women's rights, and manned polling stations to help get out the vote for transformational candidates. My husband's favorite photograph is the one of him and Bernie Sanders, just after a rally in Virginia.

My, how times have changed.

Our children have become activists, too. They can't avoid it, any more than most kids can avoid adopting the things their parents care about. Usually, however, this amounts to sports teams and hobbies, not organizing. But kids learn what they live and this is the life we lead.

Thankfully, our kids have never come to a cause through a Baptism of Fire. Our kids are not victims of crime or suffering to a degree that it captures national attention. That activism is born of blood and bone and as much as I admire kids who turn their pain into action, I wish that the world would give all children more time to be kids before their lives and illusions were so devastatingly shattered.

My kids are another kind of activist. They are emerging activists, and given their ages of 6, 7, 15, 18, and 27, they have varying degrees of awareness of what this means. Our youngest two call themselves "wildlife protectors." They will tell you everything and more than you dreamed possible about the world of animal wildlife and take actions around the house to ensure that the animal world is defended from those who would destroy it. They capture and release spiders. They've ditched straws and plastic utensils. They collect rocks and sticks and fallen feathers to add to their collection box. They are looking to see, touch, and feel the world around them.

The teenagers are much more sophisticated. They have moved beyond small, surface adjustments to their lives like ditching plastics and instead coach me and others on gender neutral language and the appropriate use of the pronoun "they." These two want to inform, influence and persuade.

And my oldest, at 27, has realized that the world is an unfair place and the most important thing he can do is be wholly and unapologetically himself. He bucks trends and loves fiercely even as many disapprove of his biracial relationship. And when he feels threatened by a political or economic policy, he finds a way to stand up for himself, and others, by doing the right thing.

All of them are somewhere on the activist continuum. Like most parents who are proud of their kids, I like to think my kids are just innately awesome. To be fair to myself and my husband, I suppose we did have a hand in shaping their views of the world. What we did isn't particularly special but it is deliberate. And it wasn't easy. Anyone who tells you raising activists is easy is selling something.

So if you are interested in raising kids who are ready to take on the problem of their community and the world, here are 10 steps to help you do it:

1. Whatever you do, make sure it is age appropriate. My husband is a passionate advocate for the planet. When he organized a two week walk to celebrate the mountains and rivers near where we lived, our daughter went along for a few days—not the whole thing. There were good times, for sure—beautiful views, amazing people, and even a kitten rescue (a fellow marcher took the wee thing home and named it "Walker" in honor of the Walk). There were also fleas, ticks, peeing in bushes, sore feet, and poor cell phone reception. She had enough of a taste to know she wanted more. You always have to leave them wanting more.

2. You have to care passionately about a cause and devote significant time and energy to achieving your vision of what the world will be like after your issue is successfully addressed. Our kids learn from our example. But don't force their participation. Rather, invite them to participate in the causes that matter to you. Before long they will either join you in your commitment or, better still, they will find their own causes. Then, do what you can to support them.

3. Don't shield them from the suffering of the world. Activism will take it out of you—this work is hard! Pain and struggle are a natural part of life and activists are on the front lines of exposing, educating, and treating the symptoms and root causes. But many parents think they can shield their children from experiencing hardship or disappointment with the world. A better approach is to immunize your kids. Expose them to small doses of injustice and suffering (again, in ways that are age appropriate) and allow their compassion to build and grow. Then, when they are exposed to a full blown case of "That Ain't Rightitis," they won't be knocked down. Instead, they will have the inner strength and resilience to tackle the issue head on.

4. Don't just fight for others—fight to change the system so that others can fight for themselves. This is important, especially if you are working on behalf of low income, disabled or other marginalized communities. Clear a path so that people at the heart of an issue can rise up and speak for and defend themselves. Share leadership. Learn the meaning of solidarity. Be willing to recongnise that their may be something to this idea of "privilege" and what that means for you and for those around you.

5. Never mind attending a rally, take them to the meetings. Activism requires showing up. This is more than becoming "woke" to the issues and showing up for the one day a year when all the cable news stations are out and everyone gets an Instagram Moment and a selfie looks really cool. Activism means showing up to collaborate with others who are addressing the issue you care about every day, right in your community. This might take up time every week over many months, if not years. There is no substitute for being present and doing the work. You need to be a reliable partner. One rally a year, even if it does blow up your newsfeed, just won't cut it.

6. Go Rally. Yes, I know what I just said. Notwithstanding that, rallies are usually a whole lot of fun besides getting you energized and motivated.

7. Be Careful Out There. Be sensible and cautious. Like the placid family dog who wouldn't hurt a fly until one day he does, rallies can be equally mercurial. What starts off as a peaceful protest or a well-crafted demonstration or prayer meeting can turn in an instant, particularly if the issue is contentious or divisive. Be on your guard, have an exit strategy and a secondary "if we get lost, here is where we will meet up" location. Write critical details like names and phone numbers in marker on your skin. Why? Because phones get confiscated by the police and lost in a shuffle. We had a friend who went to Standing Rock and was arrested at the local mall not because he was protesting but because he was looking for his wife who was in the mall shopping for camping gear and warmer clothes when a small protest was taking place. He spent the next couple of nights in jail just for being in the wrong place at the wrong time and because he looked like a protester. In Charlottesville, many folks lost their phones when crowds surged. Expect the best, but plan for the worst and don't give your kids a false sense of security. Knowledge and a plan are powerful tools.

8. Always be willing to learn from other activists, from allies, from your kids. Just when you think you have it all figured out, suddenly you find yourself trying to avoid an accident because you didn't check your blind spot. We all have them. To be an effective activist, always check your blind spot. Teach this to your kids. They will thank you for it.

9. Be in it for the long haul. Activism is hard work. It is contentious. People, even people who are right there with you in the trenches, will sometimes disagree with you. It is easy to give up, burn out, and walk away. Know your values but look for win-win solutions to complex problems. This is how you will sustain yourself and demonstrate the power of longevity to your children.

10. **Find the joy.** If activism becomes too much like hard work, you are doing it wrong. Activism is hard, yes, but it should be rewarding. You will build relationships, communities, and momentum with good people who will become like family. If at any point, you start feeling more burdened than blessed by the work, take a break. The journey is long. Keep your focus on the vision, not the problem. This is how you are able to put one foot in front of the other, day by day, week by week, and year by year. Trust that you will get there.

In looking at this list, there is a clear theme—in order to raise an activist, you need to be an activist, and not one in the mold of a Summertime Soldier, ie, a part-time soldier, serving when it's convenient. You need to be a good activist, in it for the long haul.

Like all things in life, children learn from the example that is set for them. Yes, you need to be the change you want to see in the world. That's the only way you can teach your kids to do it themselves.

Teach them well.

You'll be glad you did.

Katie is a former teacher and lawyer who currently exercises her passion for advocacy and community development by running a nonprofit on the coast of rural Maine. When not clearing obstacles so that her amazing staff can save the world one person at a time, Katie divides her time between raising five children to be educated, active, and committed citizens and finding new and creative ways to fill her cast iron dutch oven with local foods.

Katie never leaves the house without a book and 10 lipsticks in her handbag. She believes tea solves most problems and dulls the pain of the others and is happy to put the kettle on whatever the circumstances. You can reach her at katiespencerwhite@gmail.com.

KINDNESS AND GENEROSITY
MARIA DISMONDY

It was a typical Monday morning as the kids and I pulled up to a stop light on our way to the grocery store. But this time, a homeless man holding up a sign asking for help stopped us in our tracks. My 4-year-old daughter read the sign and sweetly asked why the man needed help. I explained that he was homeless and without skipping a beat, she asked, "Why doesn't he just come live with us?"

If only it were that easy, right?

It was then that I realized I needed to be proactive in exposing my children to the hard truth that there are people out there who need our help.

But I couldn't do it alone.

When I first became a mother, I searched for something to help fill the new-mom loneliness that often sets in when being home with children all day. While I'm lucky to be able to work from home, and even get out of the house a handful of times a year at speaking engagements, I was still antsy to connect with other moms in my same season of life and parenting.

My search led me to MOPS – Mothers of Preschoolers. I found a local chapter that ran out of our church with meetings held every other Monday night. They brought in speakers to talk about important topics like clean eating, marriage and parenting styles. It was such a saving grace for me to connect with these like-minded women. The sense of community and support was beyond anything I could have imagined.

Research has found that adults ranging from ages 35 to 44 are the least likely to volunteer due to time constraints. But you never would know it by looking at our MOPS crew.

A few times a year, we would use our monthly meeting to conduct a service project. One night, we made over 250 bologna sandwiches for a local shelter. Another time we packed shoeboxes for children in third world countries through an organization called Operation Shoebox. I was always blown away by the fact that a room full of women could make such a powerful difference in just an hour.

And it got me thinking about that conversation with my daughter...

I thought, "If MOPS can make it so that busy moms can take time to make a difference, why couldn't I provide the same opportunity in my home, for my children?"

A light bulb went off.

If I wanted my kids to grow up knowing that kindness and generosity did not require money but rather the use of our time, I had the power to teach this lesson at home.

Plus, I had read somewhere that providing "give back" experiences to your children and their peers can help reduce unfavorable behaviors in teens.

And so it began.

We started inviting the neighborhood kids over once a quarter to participate in service projects. Since then, we've hosted events from cereal drives to sandwich making parties to senior days at the facility across the street.

Check out the details of each event below.

Partner with a homeless shelter or some type of food bank and ask them for their food requirements. Remember that it REALLY is simple to make a difference right in your own home.

Cereal Drive - provide a list of supplies to neighborhood families for each home to sign up. Children show up with their hair tied back. Have everyone wash hands and put on gloves. Assign jobs like cereal scooper, baggie zipper, dry milk scooper, etc. We also cut out hearts from colorful construction paper for children to draw pictures on and write colorful notes. We give the hearts with the cereal and dry milk bags.

Sandwich Making Party - Similar to a cereal drive but this time the supplies are bologna, cheese, bread and mustard. We packed each sandwich into a sandwich plastic baggie then put them bag into the original bread bag before freezing. Again, with a simple sign up list for supplies, you can set up an assembly line for children to make over 100 sandwiches in one hour.

Caroling - We gather a group of families every year in December to visit our local senior home to sing holiday songs. All you need, as the organizer, is a booklet made up of songs you will sing. You can easily find these for free online. Download them and send it to your local copy shop for printing and stapling. Be sure to collect these booklets to reuse year after year. We encourage the children to communicate with the seniors on our visits to the assisted living home. Generosity, empathy and other important soft skills can come out of organized events like these!

Senior Day - Across from our neighborhood is an assisted living home. For years, we coordinated a day to visit the home with a large group of mothers and their children. I worked with the staff on dividing up roles on who provides what. We had several stations for the kids and seniors to visit: nail painting (a huge hit for the seniors who love the color of Ruby Red polish), pizza making, decorate a cookie, puzzles and card making. This is a beautiful time to get to know a senior. Sit with your child and the senior and help your child engage in the conversation. These events brought so many tears to fellow mamas as we saw the positive impact in sharing our children and time with seniors.

Cookies for Community Service Workers - Make a batch of cookies (homemade or a box mix!) and deliver them to your local police or fire station. Thank the men and women for their time and service in keeping your family safe!

Blessing Bags - Think of items that someone in need would appreciate: socks, a granola bar, hand warmers, etc. Create a wish list on Amazon and share this with your family and friends. As those boxes start showing up at your home, filled with donations, set a date for some children to plan to come over to help you unpack, organize, divide and pack items into gallon-sized zip bags. Drop them off at your local shelter for them to distribute to those in need. Some groups have packed the supplies into a backpack to deliver which is a bonus for those less fortunate and possibly living on the streets.

Award-winning author and founder of the publishing company, Cardinal Rule Press, Maria Dismondy inspires and educates others in the book industry. Maria's background in early education and research enables her to touch lives the world over while touring as a public speaker in schools, community forums, and at national conferences. When Maria isn't working, she can be found embarking on adventures throughout southeast Michigan and beyond, where she lives with her husband and three book-loving children.

THE POWER OF IN-BETWEEN TIME
SARAH O'DELL

I was eight years old when politics captured my attention. Walter Mondale had announced his pick for Vice President, Geraldine Ferraro. I was delighted. I was a young misandrist, only agreeing to read books or watch movies with girls as the main characters, only playing with other girls, and wholly convinced that boys, aside from my dad, were useless. Politics had never caught my attention because there simply weren't enough girls in it to make it seem worthwhile.

Not long after the Ferraro announcement, while I was lacing up my ice skates before my weekly lesson, I overheard someone's dad talking about voting for Reagan. Hoping to change his mind, I leaned over and said, "But if you vote for Mondale, maybe he'll DIE and we'll get to have a GIRL president!" I took this inspiring message with me to the moms and dads of my friends, no doubt winning hearts and minds for a sort-of, almost, in-case-of-emergency GIRL PRESIDENT. All I cared about was who won the big election - I was pretty disappointed, to say the least.

I lived most of my life as what I think was a pretty well-informed voter. I never missed an election, even a primary. I watched cable news with interest, attended protests, donated money to causes important to me. I admired activists who spent their whole lives dedicated to making healthcare affordable to all or talking about the climate crisis, but I had to pay back student loans and couldn't give up my life to go campaign in Iowa or whatever, so my political involvement mostly stayed in the voting booth. I still mostly cared about who won the big election.

Then I moved with my husband and two young children to New England, where every year, we vote on the town and school budget. This vote is not merely a formality, but a long, public debate about line items for copier rental costs and just how ratty and torn the carpets need to be to require replacements. I didn't understand why anyone would want to take money away from my kids' school. It was a plain, no-frills elementary school full of the kindest, most dedicated teachers and staff members I'd ever seen, all working incredibly hard. If a copier that collates the pages made their lives easier, I was all for it! I couldn't believe a reasonable person could disagree, so I started to observe closely at what was going on in my town, and what I could do to fix it.

It wasn't as easy to tackle as I thought. So many decisions impacting our lives are made at the levels of local government, and most of us have no idea what's happening at that level. As local newspapers collapse and our media outlets consolidate, folks likely have little idea what happened at the town council meeting last month unless they showed up in person. Frankly, showing up in person seemed like an impossible task for someone like me -- I was the parent in charge of most of our kids' needs while my husband worked a demanding corporate job with travel and long hours. My daughter wasn't even potty trained! I couldn't take my two fidgety kids to a Board of Education meeting at 7:30 pm on a school night, right?

Then one day I realized that the policies I was so frustrated by were created with virtually no opposition *because* of the impossibility of me getting to meetings, *because I was on my own*, juggling two kids and soccer practice and cooking dinner most nights. *Come to think of it*, virtually all the young families in the town were in the same boat. We could find an hour here or there, but not much more. The net result was that both parties had managed to install leadership that was disinterested at best, hostile at worst, to the needs and hopes that parents had. I came to understand that the fact that I and my fellow parents couldn't come speak out at a meeting was a *feature*, not a bug.

The only thing that seems to scare a politician, I knew from watching national political coverage, is the threat of losing their job. So I started showing up at meetings—and I brought my kids. It was uncomfortable A LOT of the time. My kids are talkative, fun-loving, active people. They don't have "inside voices." I was embarrassed to let them use my phone as a distraction. I was worried I'd seem like a bad mom. But I figured that letting that stop me from showing up and demanding better for our teachers and schools would arguably make me a worse mom, so I kept going. It really was just an hour here and there—I'd always thought being a political activist meant taking a leave of absence from work and riding a bus with Barack Obama, but I found that I was able to get a surprising amount of work done with the time I could manage in the space between making school lunches and chauffeuring to soccer practice. You can call a lot of folks in a phone bank, you can write a lot of postcards to friends asking them to support a budget, and you can set up a Facebook page and schedule a few posts—all in just an hour. And when everyone is using their "in-between" time, it adds up.

I came to understand that far from making me a *bad* mom, dragging my kids around to League of Women Voter debates and putting up lawn signs was making me a *better* mom. I found myself getting into more substantive discussions about our family values and what being a good citizen looks like. My son listened to the coverage of the 2018 midterms, asking, "How are they going to make sure every kid gets to go to a nice school? I didn't hear them mention kids!"

I started wondering what else this kind of here-and-there hands-on action could accomplish. I noticed our local state senator had voted against confirming a judge because he was gay, and she'd sponsored a bill that would have taken away rights from parents to have input on kids' IEPs. I decided I'd spend a little time volunteering for the campaign of her challenger. When a friend-of-a-friend announced he was running for state representative, I wanted to support him, too. Yet another friend asked me if I might help her out with a campaign a few towns away—she just needed a little help to get the word out about her candidate in what was shaping up to be a close race. I said yes to all of it, and more. A few hours here and there, spread between campaigns…it wasn't much. I certainly don't think I was the factor that made the difference. But when I zipped in for a phone bank after a quick dinner with the kids, I looked down the packed table and saw it filled with mostly women -- from seniors my mom's age to girls in high school who couldn't even vote yet, most of us strangers to each other—crushing call lists and laughing. The power of our "in-between" time was changing the political landscape.

What I want every mom to know is that naptime can be your power hour. You can take the kids for a walk through the neighborhood with their friends while you knock on doors for someone you believe in. You don't need to give up your life, you don't need to hire a nanny, you don't need to quit your job. You can change the world by sending emails asking your friends to show up at a debate while you're crossing town on the subway. You can show up at your congressman's district office during your lunch hour. You can organize a fundraiser for a great candidate during your kid's swim lesson.

I didn't know how little I could do and make such a big difference, and I wish I'd started sooner. I guess a lot of us busy parents do these days, given where the country is now. Voting isn't enough, and saying the right thing on social media isn't enough, and it's a lesson my kids are already taking in. And, in a turn that would have delighted my 8 year old self, seeing the everyday power of women working together has my preschool aged daughter pretty convinced that politics are, as she'd say, "for GIRLS."

Sarah O'Dell is a social media consultant, activist and mom who currently lives in Connecticut but never fails to mention she's from Pittsburgh. After earlier lives in nonprofit fundraising and human resources, she spends her professional and personal time trying to make the world a better, nicer, fairer place, and also knitting.

THE EXAMPLES WE SET
YVONNE MARCUS

When I was a child, we passed by a church and my cousin said she was a Christian. I looked up and said "I'm not. I'm a 'Publican."

I identified myself with my political affiliation, because it was the political affiliation of one of the most important people in my life, my pappaw. I listened carefully to everything he told me, and I took it to heart. He's the reason I knew I was a Republican.

Listen, I wrote a letter to the President of the United States when I was 5 years old. I wrote about how I was Republican. I only knew one Democrat. And the President, he was the best Republican. President George H.W. Bush sent me a letter back.

I had dessert in the Congressional dining room (ice cream) and took a private tour of Congress that same year, because I was a proud Republican.

My entire family went to the polls, at my elementary school, every election day. Yes, they even voted in every local election. I remember running out of line to hug my pappaw or my Uncle Claude before they went to cast their vote.

My elementary school principal, Mr. Bob Martin, remembers seeing me at the polls myself no less than 3 times a day during any given election. I'd go with my nana when I got home from school, my aunt when she got home from work, and my mom later. To me, voting was a requirement of being a citizen.

I learned by example.

Most children learn things by the examples they are given in their lives. This same idea goes for the political process.

My pappaw's restaurant was the town gathering spot. It was the place the locals came to debate politics.

I remember many a moment of my Uncle Claude getting heated over something our local officials were doing, but I have no recollection of it every being personal. I remember the same men and women would meet on those stools every morning to discuss politics and the latest town gossip. Honestly, I don't remember a lot of minds getting changed on their end, but it left a seed in the young minds who happened to stop by.

As a young child, I learned to always show up and vote. I learned how to form my own political opinions, and I learned to debate. As I grew, I learned that those debates about local politics were some of the most important debates to be had, because it was those political races and decisions that would have the largest impact on my daily life. These are the decisions that determine where money will be spent in your community.

Does the street where three accidents happened last week need a traffic light?

Is there money in the budget for that?

Can we build a sidewalk downtown so that people can walk freely without worry of traffic?

What are the logistics of that? Can Uber operate in your town?

Airbnb?

These things are not usually determined by the state or national government. They are often decided by your local mayor and commissioners.

Did you vote in your last local election?

If you didn't, you aren't alone. Big national elections draw the most attention and thus get the largest voter turnout, but these elections were often a reminder for me to bring it back to the local level.

My nana would say that she wouldn't vote for some big politician if he were running for dog catcher, and I'd laugh. Truthfully though, the dog catcher would have more impact on our daily lives than that senator, so it was definitely a telling statement (although it also implies that dog catching is an easy job).

The truth is, your vote matters. I know you've heard that your whole lives, and you've grown to believe it isn't really truth. Yet, I'll tell you again that your vote matters.

Your vote matters because my nana wouldn't vote for so-and-so for dog catcher. Your vote matters because my pappaw taught me I was a Republican long before I knew I was a Christian. Your vote matters because local elections have a smaller number of voices determining the outcome and the outcome of those elections does more to your daily life than any other.

Your vote matters because little eyes are watching.

So, let's talk about some of the ways your local elected officials affect your daily life.

Your town likely has a property tax that can range anywhere from 0-4% of your properties value. This money is often used to fund local or state programs so you likely you are fine with paying this tax. However, if you don't feel like they're spending your money wisely, you will likely want to vote for someone who either aligns with your spending desires or wants to reduce the amount. You can only affect this during a local election.

Would you like to take an Uber or Lyft to the airport?

This is absolutely something that is determined on the local level. My city recently decided to charge a fee to Uber/Lyft drivers for pick-up/drop off at the local airport. This can make it difficult for people who want to fly from that airport due to the difficulty of finding someone to take them to catch their flight or pick them up on their return. It also hampers tourists getting to and from the airport. The cost of long-term parking at the airport can also be prohibitive.

Do you love staying in an Airbnb?

Airbnb in my town has racked up almost $1M in fines for some local homeowners. If you live in my city, you should know it's a $500/day fine for renting your house or apartment out as a short-term rental. That adds up quickly in this tourist destination. If we want to change that law, we will need to vote for city officials who are willing to be supportive of short-term rentals.

Do you feel like the speed limit is too high in your residential area?

The state determines speed limits for your area. Recently in my area, the speed limit was reduced near my house due to too many accidents. This was a blessing considering the types of accidents I have seen there. But if I hadn't voted for officials who cared about the lives of their constituents, we could still be seeing people flying down that path of roadway.

Voting in local elections is vital. It is what keeps your community running smoothly. It may also be what attracts new people to your area.

Local government creates infrastructure for your city. It invites or rejects innovation and jobs. It takes your tax dollars and reinvests them in your community directly.

When I was a child, my local government decided to institute a forced busing procedure. This meant that it was going to take an hour each way for me to get home via the bus. Also, we were forced to move our bus stop from the bottom of my driveway to about half a mile down the road. It was determined that even young children could walk this far to catch the bus. My road was the longest secondary road in the US with semi-trucks constantly zooming down it. Also, it had no sidewalks. This meant I could not reasonably walk to the bus stop.

Our neighbor literally kept calling the school board and the superintendent of schools to get this situation rectified. It was a middle of the night phone call that was finally the wake-up call to them about how important this issue was to our community.

The community and voters are absolutely vital to change.

The best way to teach your children about these elections and how it affects their life is to talk to them about it. Trust them with the information and let them form their own opinions. For a while, they will agree with you wholeheartedly. Allow them to begin to debate so that they will learn how to stand up for their community and their own beliefs. This was a vital part of my childhood. I saw political debate happen in that small, country restaurant, amongst my family, and later amongst my friends. I was taught how to do it politely and without name calling.

This is how we build a better tomorrow.

Yvonne Marcus is currently based in Asheville, North Carolina, where she is a wife to Jeremy and a mom to Lil Sprout and Squeakers. Her life's passion is to help moms. She knows that we all feel pressure to do #allthethings, but she knows that we also know that's just not feasible. We should have the life we want, though, and she's glad to say that she's living that life. She quit her job to pursue my dream of Yvonne Marcus Consulting as soon as she found out Lil Sprout was on the way. It might have seemed a little premature, but she was definitely tired of that two-hour commute to work every day. Can you blame her? Her hope is that she'll be able to help you live that life as well, your best life.

TAKE YOUR CHILDREN WITH YOU
ALEXA BIGWARFE

There was a time when my children were small and I often skipped voting in the midterm elections. I had a lot of excuses - no one to watch the kids, I didn't want to stand in line with them being nuts all around me, Midterms weren't important anyway.

Wait, what?

Now it's hard to believe that I thought ANY of those things. I was at home with my children, but I'm sure there are plenty of working moms who have also run their list of excuses around voting. If we've learned anything over the last several years, it should be that it is important for us to show up and vote EVERY TIME we get the opportunity.

I have changed my mindset a bit on this. I understand that we have to show up and cast our votes… that they are ALL important. And if I can't find a sitter, I have options. One, I can take the kids with me. More about that in a minute.

Secondly, I can vote early. Most cities now have an early voting option, and where I live, being the primary care giver of children is an accetpable reason for voting early. I haven't done my research on this entirely, but I believe you don't even have to have a reason to vote early anymore in most places - you just go vote early. But skipping an election, for me at least, is never an option any more.

Midterms are tremendously important.

First of all, any number of national spots are being elected/re-elected and it's a fantastic time to get rid of the people who have been there for too long or no longer support or help women and mothers by their policies and voting records.

Secondly, so many VERY important local and state elections occur during the midterms. We're voting for our governor, my state representatives, and our school board in this election. These are all tremendously important.

Third - bonds, referendums, and local tax/policy issues. We have numerous key issues on the ballot, as I'm sure you do too.

As my children grow older, I realize just how important those school board seats are. I understand that the local taxes, bonds, and other referendums truly have an impact on my day-to-day life.

Women's issues are suffering because more women don't show up.

Reproductive health issues, gender wage gaps, protections in the workplace, paid sick leave and other healthcare initiatives... these are so critical to us as women, as mothers, but they aren't going to be addressed if we aren't ensuring that candidates who are willing to talk about and support these initiatives are elected.

We have a large problem in this country with apathy and expecting that things will just work out. The problem is, they don't just "work out". Rights are being stripped, fascism and racism are growing, it feels like we're moving backward on many gender and rights issues... we can no longer sit on the sidelines quietly and just hope for the best.

But voting is only one part of the equation.

As engaged mothers, we need to also raise our children to understand how important it is to be a part of the process, to use their voices, to speak up about the issues that impact them, and to make sure they are backing the people and the policies that support those agendas. It's my opinion that we need to raise children that are comfortable discussing issues and public policy without resorting to anger and arguments. And this will come more naturally if they are raised believing that discussing issues is normal and important.

TIPS FOR TEACHING YOUR CHILDREN TO BE PART OF THE PROCESS:

Model the behavior. The best way to teach them the importance is to show them. Take them with you to the polls. I took my kids with me to the last election. I suppose one of the benefits of low voter turnout is that there was absolutely no line. I had no issues walking right in and was casting my vote within 5 minutes. I even let the girls click on the boxes for me. They got stickers to show they "voted" and they understood the significance of being part of the process. The line is not always short. Plan accordingly. Do not take the children with you in high traffic times (first thing in the morning, lunchtime, or after work) unless you are prepared with activities. Some voting sites will move women with small children to the front of the line, but not all. If you can't take the children with you, make sure you get your sticker and tell them you voted. Show them you voted and let them know WHY you voted.

Talk about the issues. Obviously, we don't have to get into the details on reproductive rights and hot topic issues with the kids, unless you really want to, but it is important that they understand why voting is important. Why it matters who is elected, and what the governmental process is like. There are many resources - books, websites, educational programming, that can help you teach it at their level if you aren't sure how to do this.

Take them to rallies or other events. In 2019, I plan on taking my girls to the Women's March. I have taken them to events hosted by Moms Demand Action. It's usually quite fun and opens many doors for conversation. It does make me a little nervous, and honestly, I may only take my older daughter. I'm a little nervous that I will get caught up in the excitement and literally lose my 6-year-old. That would not be good. Also, I'm not sure she'd really understand the message. But my older daughter is ready to learn from these types of activities. I think it will leave a long-lasting impression on her.

Try to remove emotion and anger from the discussion. This one is tough, I know! I remember one day I said something about Trump, and my six-year-old screamed, "Trump!?! I HATE

Trump!" While I thought it was a little funny, I also felt embarrassed. I want to raise children that are thoughtful and deliberate, but I don't want the discussion to be hateful. It's especially hard in certain circumstances, but I subscribe to the old southern saying, "You kill more flies with sugar than vinegar". (Say that with a strong, southern drawl, y'all.) But it's true. Anger and emotion just lead to more anger and emotion. No one learns, listens, or changes based on that approach. Instead, talk about the issues, the legislation. Why is it important? What does it mean? How can we impact change?

Involve them in community activities. We raise money for organizations that are important for us, we do walks and runs and charity events that help organizations and causes, we serve the needs of our community. And I can see my children impacted for life when each time they participate. As a child, my parents took me to serve in Soup Kitchens and deliver meals and items to homeless or needy families. These actions drilled into me a sense of compassion, desire to help others, and a realization of how much our family had in comparison to others. We did not have a lot, by the way, but more than many. To this day, my heart is bigger, which leads me to continue to advocate on the behalf of those who are marginalized.

The list could go on, but I find these to be a great place to start. Don't get overwhelmed in the process. Find what works for you, and go with it.

If we want to raise involved kids, we have to show them what it means to be a part of the process. And taking them with us is a fantastic way to do it.

Alexa Bigwarfe is a loud advocate for those without a voice. She is a USA Today Best Selling Author, an author coach, and a publisher. She coaches others through the self-publishing process at writepublishsell.com. She started blogging as an outlet for her grief after the loss of one of her twin daughters to Twin to Twin Transfusion Syndrome (TTTS) and now uses the blog to advocate for those without a voice. She is also the founder of LoseTheCape.com, and is the editor and publisher of the Lose the Cape! series. The mother of three wildlings, Alexa spends her free time coming up with ways to try to save the world from her home in Columbia, SC and drags her children along for the ride.

TEACH YOUR CHILDREN WELL: HOW RAISING ACTIVISTS CAN NOT ONLY MAKE THE WORLD BETTER, IT CAN IMPROVE CHILDREN'S LIVES

GRETCHEN KELLY

Raising tiny humans is not for the faint of heart. We worry and fret over their health, their social lives, their interests, their future. To parent is to spend sleepless nights worried over things we can and can't control. When the world feels like it's spinning backwards and chaos seems the new norm, this worry is amplified. It can leave us feeling helpless, wondering what kind of world our children will inherit.

The best way to combat despair and helplessness is action. And as much as we may try to protect our children from the uglier side of the news, the truth is they hear and see and absorb more than we realize. The older they get, the more they are aware. And those who are able to live without fear of discrimination or harm or subjugation are indeed the lucky few.

But maybe protecting them is not the answer. Maybe filtering the world and the news is giving them a false sense of reality that will not serve them well when reality comes crashing in. Maybe... maybe using what's happening in the world to teach them how to be better humans is exactly what we should be doing. It will make their lives richer, more fulfilling. And beyond the good it does for their character, fighting discrimination and racism and all forms of oppression can have ripple effects throughout their lives. It can make them better citizens, yes. But it can also teach them how to have healthy relationships, how to navigate the world and how to do better in their endeavors.

Raise them to consider the world around them and you will be giving them the tools to be successful, to have good relationships and to navigate the world in a positive way.

Teach them that Impact is greater than Intent. Teach them about how the imbalance of power is almost always a conduit for abuse. Teach them that apathy is dangerous.

IMPACT > INTENT

"The road to hell is paved with best intentions"
- Ancient proverb of unknown origin

Impact is greater than intent.

Every single school and corporate motto can and should be whittled down to this simple phrase. Make it a common refrain in your home. Teach it to your children. Tattoo it on your forehead and print it on a bumper sticker.

This phrase, or some version of it, comes up a lot in activism. It is a succinct way of saying that sometimes we hurt others, even when we didn't mean to. It highlights the ways that implicit racism and sexism and bigotry cause real harm even when no harm is intended. Impact is key. Impact is what matters. When it comes to biases, the death of a thousand cuts is often done with no bad intentions. The subtle, underlying prejudices that are invisible to those who carry them are the most insidious. We are all guilty of saying something without realizing the harm in our words. We've all bought into assumptions or ideas about other groups of people without considering that they myth is false and that our assumptions add to oppression.

We're not all bigots casting off hateful words and actions without a care. We have all, unknowingly, unintentionally hurt others. This is the byproduct of a racist and sexist society. It's virtually impossible to be immersed in it from birth and not absorb it and unwittingly adopt it. Talking about impact mattering more than intent is not meant to blame or to shame. It's meant to awaken. To remove the blinders you didn't even know you were wearing. Once you're awake and the blinders are off, you see it. You start to recognize it. You start to listen instead of scoffing at terms like "micro-aggressions." You start to realize that innocuous, innocent words and actions actually can harm others. That your impact can feel like a brutal blow without realizing you'd even thrown a punch.

Impact > Intent can be applied to school, work, community, and relationships. Teaching your children this vital component of activism can bleed into all areas of their lives. Once your children start to read the world with clearer comprehension, they will see that their intent is only half of the equation.

Their intention may be to ace the test. But if they didn't study as rigorously as they should have, they will fail. Your daughter may not have intended to hurt her friend, but if she laughed at a cruel joke at her friend's expense, the friend hurts just the same.

Flirting with a girl who's walking down the hall may seem innocent enough to your son, but if he ignores her body language because he's caught up in his feelings or nervousness, he may make her feel very uncomfortable in ways he never intended.

In relationships impact vs intent plays itself out on a daily basis. Our own perceptions and baggage and life experiences bump up against the one we love in ways that can be incredibly hurtful and damaging without us even realizing it. One person's fear of abandonment can make the other feel smothered and controlled. One person's stress or exhaustion can feel like detachment to the one they love. Healthy relationships can rise and fall based on how much we pay attention to the impact of our actions. Focusing only on our intent dismisses the hurts and the needs of our loved ones. When you love someone you try to see things from their perspective as well as your own, and the best relationships mean understanding each other's perspective and minimizing the damage of subconscious actions and words.

Beyond "do no harm" and "do unto others," intentions should be about self-awareness, about how every word and action can have a ripple effect and touch others. Focusing on intentions, when your actions have hurt someone is selfish and counterproductive. Crying "but I meant…" is to ignore those you harmed and to deflect from the real issue.

Teaching this to your children is crucial to their relationships. Teaching this is crucial to their success in the workplace. And teaching it to them when it comes to cultural and societal ills is vital to our humanity. It's all about raising good humans. We want them to be successful in life, to have great relationships and marriages and friendships. But don't we also want them to bring more good to this world? To leave it a little better than it was? Teaching them impact > intent is one of the most effective ways to give them a push in the right direction on all those fronts. And you can start teaching it when they are young.

When we teach Impact > Intent, we are teaching our children life skills. When they see us putting it to practice- by doing something to help others, by fighting injustice instead of just lamenting it- we are demonstrating it. Showing up for our communities and our neighbors and especially to fight inequality, teaches them humanity. It teaches them that they can be agents of change. That progress only happens when people get involved. It teaches them that the world is bigger than them, that the needs of others are always worth considering and fighting for.

It makes them better people.

It can protect them from making life altering mistakes.

It can enable them to have better, healthier relationships

Teach your children that impact is ALWAYS key, their intentions are only part of the story.

POWER STRUCTURES

"Power tends to corrupt, and absolute power corrupts absolutely"
- John Dalber-Acton

As a parent, one of the things I worry about the most is abuse. I know that "stranger danger" is an overblown idea. The idea of a stranger hurting our child strikes fear in the heart of every parent, but abuse rarely comes from strangers. Most often comes from people we know. And it is almost always about power structures and the imbalance of power.

Power imbalance comes in many forms. It's sometimes harmless and a simple fact of life. But when power is concentrated with the wrong person or people it can be incredibly dangerous.

In activism we focus on the imbalance of power, especially when there are no checks on that power. When we see a police force with no oversight and toxic leadership, we see more abuse of marginalized citizens. When private prisons are unregulated, modern day slavery is the result. When mega churches grow their coffers with hard-earned tithes, sometimes men of God buy private jets and live in McMansions while those they profess to help are left wanting.

There's a reason we have three branches of government and a free press is protected by the Constitution. Because controlling the most powerful country in the world is a heady thing that can lead to abuse if not checked. There's a reason there are Human Resources Departments to ensure that employees are treated fairly. There's a reason there are unions and oversight committees and Child Protective Services. Because people in positions of power, whether in government or the workplace or schools or caretakers of young children, need to be held accountable and those who hold little or no power need to be protected. It's critical to a healthy, functioning democracy and society.

To fight for equality, for better healthcare, for voting rights, or to stop the oppression of a group of people, we are fighting power structures that have run rampant. Our protest and boycotts, our phone calls to congress, all of these actions are a check on power. There will always be power grabs. It's our job to make sure that we grab back. When our children see us doing this, they see that we are not helpless in the face of the powerful. They see that there is strength in knowledge and awareness and numbers. We teach them to fight for the rights of the powerless. And in the process, we can teach them how to make sure they are never the victim of the powerful.

This may be one of the most empowering things you can teach your kids. Teach them to recognize when power is concentrated with no restraints. Teach them to see that when marginalized people have no recourse, that is an abuse of power. Teach them all the shapes and forms that abusive power comes in.

When you raise your child to be an activist, you will show them how to fight and recognize the large and obvious power structures. But you can also alert them to the less obvious. The more subtle forms of power, the everyday abuses. The abuse that can happen at work, at school, at home, in their relationships.

A teacher that belittles a student to embarrass and shame. A boss who crosses the line with offensive jokes or inappropriate contact. A husband that controls the finances as a way of controlling his wife. A wife who uses manipulation to control her husband. A man who won't take no when it comes to dating or intimacy. A group of students at a party pressuring a kid to drink. A man slipping a drug into a woman's drink. All of these are abuses of power. Or deliberate use of devices to gain power in order to abuse. And all can be demoralizing at best and devastating at worst.

Power and abuse show up in our everyday lives in so many ways. The sooner your children start to recognize it, the sooner they can call it out or avoid it or fight it. Teach them that the abusers are counting on no one checking their power. Empower and show them how to bankrupt the abuser's power. Engaging in activism gives us all the confidence that we can fight abuse and the power structures that enable it. You can't fight what you don't see. Recognize the abuse of power in all it's forms. When someone hits a dog, point out that they are using their power to hurt. When a bully picks on the smallest kid, point out how weak the bully's power really is. That his power lies only in the willingness of bystanders to do nothing.

Teaching your children about power structures and how it's used to abuse is the best protection you can offer them. Not only can they be a stick in the wheel of unchecked power, but they can spot it from afar and avoid it when it comes to their own life.

APATHY

"I have a very strong feeling that the opposite of love is not hate- it's apathy."

- Dr. Leo Buscaglia

Noun: apathy 1. lack of interest, enthusiasm, or concern.

Apathy is a void. A lack of. Nothing good comes from apathy. In fact, apathy can be dangerous.

Apathy is what causes roughly 46 percent of eligible voters in the U.S. to not vote. Apathy is what has a populace shrugging when civil rights are violated. Apathy allows us to not pay attention to what is happening beyond our front door. Or our street. Or our country. Apathy is an affliction of the privileged. Or the plight of the oppressed who've had the fight beaten out of them. Or the surrender of the exhausted.

Apathy is one of the biggest killers of marriage. Apathy can lead to job loss. Decline in health. Stagnant careers. Loss of drive and creativity and hope. And if you've ever suffered from severe depression, you know that apathy can kill.

Apathy enables genocide. Authoritarianism. Killing of innocent people. Apathy is what allows children to be locked in cages in the name of border security and allowed Jews to be put in ghettos. Apathy shrugs at red flags and warning signs. It looks the other way when loss of freedoms creep in slowly. Apathy sees horrors happening on cell phone recordings or to people who don't look like us or talk like us and decides it can't happen to us. Apathy tells us lies like "he should have listened to the police" or "they shouldn't have come illegally" or "they are coming for your jobs." Apathy relies on lies. It whispers lies to moderates while they sleep, a lullaby of indifference.

The disinterest in the suffering of others is something to behold. We all have our pet causes and our passions. But when we see our government commit atrocities, it's time to join in the pet cause of NOT ON MY WATCH. When children are taken from their parents and put in cages, it's time for us to all shake off any apathy we may be clinging to. And it's just as important that we make sure our kids aren't growing up so sheltered that they are oblivious to what is going on around them. Insulating them from the realities happening outside their front door is dangerous to them and to society.

It's the conundrum of the privileged parent. How much do I expose my children? How much do I tell them about bad things happening to good people? Do I let them see what's happening on the evening news? This answer is different for every parent because every child is different. We must take into account what our children are going through. A child already struggling with crippling anxiety or depression probably needs to be shielded from upsetting news. A child who is chronically sick may need to focus on positive energy and healing. And parents who are struggling with sick children or who are struggling to make it to the next paycheck probably aren't able to spend any time or energy on activism. That is fine, that is why those of us who can, should. It's why those who have the time or energy or capital take up the cause. And when we need a break or they have a crisis, someone else is there to take the baton. This is a relay, not a solo cross country.

Teach your children to take the baton and run with it. To pass it when they need to attend to themselves.

Make your children aware of the good and the bad in the world. Show them how to fight the bad and celebrate the good. Don't let apathy infect your home. Teach them that you fight for things that matter. Fight for your health, your education, your relationships, the people you care about. That you fight for your rights and if your rights aren't being threatened, you fight for those whose are.

Raising your kids to be activists teaches them to not be

bystanders, not when it comes to a cause that matters to them and not in their own lives.

It teaches them that apathy only serves those who want to control. It is the tool of abusers and tyrants. It is the opposite of love.

***

Being involved in activism doesn't have to be a solo mission. There is community in activism. And raising your children to be a part of this community can be a beautiful thing. There is inclusivity, broadening of world views, understanding of hardships others endure, and a sense of loving not only one's neighbors but all people. It's living a life that isn't about "I got mine" but about "how can we do this together."

Activism can give your children tools for life. It can equip them with knowledge that protects them from abuse and allows them to better understand the impact they have on the world. It can teach them to fight for what's right and to always see that there's a way to justice.

It teaches them that love wins.

That there is more good than bad in this world.

That when people come together, amazing things can happen.

That hope is always worth clinging too.

It teaches them that love does, in fact, trump hate.

Gretchen Kelly is a writer, activist, and mom of three. Social justice is the main driver of her writing. In addition to feminism and politics, she writes about grief, parenting, and random musings on life. She has appeared in Upworthy, Huffington Post, Scary Mommy, Elephant Journal, and was a featured writer and cohost of the Stop Sexism podcast for the Good Men Project.

Twitter: https://twitter.com/gkelly73
FB: https://www.facebook.com/driftingthrough/

TEACHING YOUR CHILDREN ABOUT INEQUALITIES AROUND GENDER, RACE AND CULTURE

LAURA LYLES REAGAN

The American immigration system is in flux, to put it lightly. Parents and children are still being separated at the border of Texas and Mexico despite the fact that the courts mandated the administration to halt the policy. The private prison systems continue to profit from detention centers or the incarceration rate of our population, usually persons of color. The divide between rich and poor in our country is growing ever larger. There is no greater issue before us, politically, than inequality.

It is so easy to become overwhelmed by the inequities we see and hear reported every day. It's hard not to lose heart and remember we can take the greatest actions in the smallest of ways at home, with the children we are shaping into productive members of society. As the news and rhetoric around racial and ethnic issues heat up, perhaps it's time to reflect on what messages we want to send our kids. These seem like weighty topics to tackle with kids, yet children are exposed daily to our country's struggle with race and culture. So, what is the best way to help children sort through these issues, develop the values of empathy, equality and fairness, while learning to engage, speak up and be heard?

1. PRACTICE DIVERSITY. BE A GOOD RACE AND GENDER RELATIONS ROLE MODEL.

Behaviorists tell us that the first rule of thumb is to model the behavior you want. We can demonstrate positive race relations in practical ways in our own lives. Do you have friends of other races? If most of your friends are from your own race and culture, you may want to consider opportunities for you and your child to interact with others from diverse backgrounds. One idea is to attend a different place of worship for a day. Observe the service together and find something to appreciate about it. Then comment about it to your child. If you see a television program about a different culture, use the opportunity to discuss different ways of life and worldviews. Find one thing you like about the culture you are observing, and state it out loud.

2.) BE INTENTIONAL. BE VERBAL.

Activist mindsets often begin by developing critical thinking about the hidden fears and agendas we project. When a sexy commercial with a woman barely dressed and draped over a car is shown, comment about it. Ask why a man wasn't used as a model. Or when a commercial for a cleaning product only shows the mom mopping, talk about it as a stereotype. Discuss what stereotypes mean.

3.) REMEMBER TO LISTEN. DON'T ASSUME SHARED UNDERSTANDINGS. MINDFULLY WATCH FOR TEACHABLE MOMENTS.

Sociologist assert that children construct differences and similarities differently than adults and they have their own agency. That means kids are co-creating meaning from the social world every day. Children notice differences quite early, but it may be for reasons apparent only to children, and not to adults, who may notice something different. A teacher noticed that six-year-old girls on a playground were not playing with one girl in particular, who was African American. The astute teacher listened first before intervening and found that the majority of the girls preferred to play with girls who wore their hair with ribbons instead of girls who didn't use ribbons.

The African American girl didn't use ribbons in her hair. She was excluded from conversations and games. The girls were not excluding her because of race, but because of ribbons. To adult eyes, the game looked racist, but to the children controlling the game, it made sense. The teacher then noticed one girl sharing her ribbons with the African American girl. The teacher wisely chose to call attention to that moment and praised the sharing behavior. It opened up an opportunity to discuss inclusion.

3.) ANSWER YOUR CHILD'S QUESTIONS ABOUT RACE AND CULTURE IN AN AGE APPROPRIATE WAY.

Psychiatrist Alvin Poussaint, M.D., shared that there are two critical developmental periods when race and culture questions are likely to occur. They are, ages six to eight years old, and the teenage years. These stages are times when the child's world is expanding and their values are forming or solidifying. Responding to a child's questions at these stages in simple, honest terms is important. Even a response of "I don't know" or "let's read about that" can show you are open to learning about different cultures, customs and communities.

When your child comes home and declares a classmate has an Asian mom and a black dad and says, "Isn't that weird?" You may choose to say, "Not weird, just different." When your teen asks what you think about his school renaming their sports teams because Native Americans find "Redskins" to be offensive, you can use it as an opportunity to discuss your own beliefs about racial slurs while demonstrating respect that others might not see it the same way.

Perhaps we can heed now more than ever, Dr. Martin Luther King's last Christmas sermon. "The Christmas hope for peace and goodwill toward all men can no longer be dismissed as a kind of pious dream of some utopia. If we don't have good will toward men in this world, we will destroy ourselves by the misuse of our own instruments and our own power." If we heed Dr. King's words, vision and example, we can intervene on the divisions in the nation, in our own homes, every day.

There are many resources for parents desiring to discuss raise and diversity with their kids. If you need help with talking about these issues with your kids, there are many resources, including the following:

www.tolerance.org

bouncebackparenting.com/resources-for-talking-to-kids-about-race-and-racism

Raceconscious.org

Laura Lyles Reagan holds a Masters of Science in Sociology. She's spent over 30 years working as a passionate community advocate, specializing in child and youth advocacy, mentoring, youth development, academic success models, parenting, and family poverty issues. She's a professional parenting coach, writer, and speaker.

CONCLUSION

Wait! We're only getting started! Do you feel fired up yet and ready to get involved? Hopefully we've demonstrated that being involved can look different to all of us, but it is indeed important to do something.

We don't live in the same world we did once-upon-a-time, where we could sit back and expect that the system was working for us. It's critical, especially as we try to make the world better for women and children, that we use our voices, that we step up, that we do something… and that we teach our children how important it is for them to be involved as well.

Our elected officials are still over 70 percent male. We need women's voices. We need leadership. We need moms. We need the future generation that moms are raising.

We need momvocates!

WHAT IS A MOMVOCATE?

I think most moms are momvocates, even if they don't know it. In some way, shape, or form, we all advocate on a daily basis for whatever is in the best interest of our children. A "momvocate" just takes it to the next level by trying to affect change on a level that impacts more than just her own children. Whether this is volunteering with an organization, writing letters to leadership for change, trying to pass legislation, spreading information about a topic to bring more awareness, fundraising and supporting a cause, and so forth, a Momvocate takes those issues she is passionate about and brings them to the forefront. We hope our stories have inspired you to use your voice too! Moms can make a loud roar!

Are you ready to join the movement? #whyImomvocate #momsvoices

"IF THEY DON'T GIVE YOU A SEAT AT THE TABLE, BRING A FOLDING CHAIR."

— SHIRLEY CHISHOLM, THE FIRST AFRICAN AMERICAN WOMAN ELECTED TO CONGRESS

SPECIAL INVITATION

We want you to be part of our Lose the Cape tribe! If you're interested in joining our Mom Squad group, we invite you to oin us here: https://www.facebook.com/groups/YourMomSquad/

If you write about motherhood and want to contribute to the Lose the Cape blog, please email us your submission at info@losethecape.com.

Be sure to check out our podcast - http://losethecape.com/podcast or find us on Itunes or Stitcher.

Let's get social! Please follow us here:

Facebook: Facebook.com/LoseTheCape

Twitter at twitter.com/LosetheCape

Instagram: instagram.com/LosetheCape

Pinterest: pinterest.com/LosetheCape

Finally, if you've enjoyed this book, we hope you'll visit us on Amazon and/or GoodReads and leave us a raving review. This will help other parents find us too!

ABOUT THE EDITORS

Alexa Bigwarfe is a freelance writer, mother of three children, and a dog owner. In addition to raising her children, managing her home, and writing, Alexa's heart is in advocacy and raising funds to support nonprofit organizations involved with infant, children and women's issues. Alexa launched her writing with her personal blog No Holding Back, (katbiggie.com). Here she chronicles topics including health and wellness, living with autoimmune diseases, and most importantly, her grief after the loss of one of her twin daughters to complications from Twin to Twin Transfusion Syndrome (TTTS). Alexa took the experience from that painful life event and channeled it into a compilation book for grieving mothers entitled *Sunshine After the Storm: A Survival Guide for the Grieving Mother*. In addition to the Lose the Cape series, she has been published in multiple other anthologies and several books on the topic of writing and publishing, including *Ditch the Fear and Just Write It!*. (Download your free copy at www.writepublishsell.co/dtf) Alexa enjoys helping other authors get their important words into the world as well through her company Write|Publish|Sell. In her "spare" time, you can find Alexa enjoying time with her girlfriends or hiding in her closet for some "alone" time.

Nancy Cavillones enjoys taking the scenic route, forcing her kids to appreciate nature, and spending time in New York City by herself in a desperate attempt to recapture her college days. Nancy recently relocated to Northern California with her family, where she hopes sweater weather exists. She is Managing Editor of *Lose the Cape* and co-host of the Lose The Cape podcast.

http://therealnani.com

ACKNOWLEDGEMENTS

We want to thank the contributors who were brave enough to share their voices for this book. Thank you for sharing your laughs, your wisdom and your personal experiences and for being open to talk about a topic that is not always easily and readily received in today's world.

We'd like to give a big shout out to the women we've turned to in 2020 to learn how to be better supporters of women of color and help change the dialogue in the country: Desiree Peterkin Bell, Roshanda Pratt, E. Danielle Butler, Nikia Bristow, Nina Thomas Estwick, Bellamy Shoffner, to name a few of the women who've had such a great impact on us. Thank you.

We'd also like to thank our faithful, always honest and diverse Lose the Cape community. Thank you for engaging with us on the blog, in social media, for listening to our podcasts and for reading our books. We strive to create a space where all parents feel accepted and safe to share. Your energy, sense of humor and kindness are evident in every interaction we have with you. Truly, you are AH-MAZING! We love our peeps.

This book would have taken years more to complete had it not been for the help of our team. Adrienne Hedger—once again, your cover design knocked it out of the park! Michelle Fairbanks—the graphics were ON POINT! Thanks for taking Adrienne's incredible artwork and running with it. And Raewyn Sangari—your support and social media expertise is a crucial part of our daily business.

I (Alexa) would like to thank my Wolf Pack - Jody Smith, Cristin Downs, Katie Hanus, and Julie Neale - the discussions that we have had on this topic of being enganged and raising children that are engaged and involved in the process have been invaluable to me. I can't wait to see all of the amazing things that we will do in the upcoming years.

And finally, we would be remiss to not thank our families. Without your support, none of this is even a thing. Without our children, there is is no discussion on motherhood. And without our spouses supporting us to follow these dreams... well, it'd be a really difficult road to navigate. Love you always.

IF YOU DO NOT WALK IN THE DOOR, YOU WILL NOT GET INVOLVED.

— JEN ROSEN HEINZ

RESOURCES

For Moms

Momsrising.org is a fantastic place to start when trying to learn about current issues that impact women and mothers, and find easy ways to get involved.

Moms Demand Action: https://momsdemandaction.org/

Hold the Line Magazine: https://htlmagazine.com/

Poltical Resources

To help you find out who your elected officials are, go here: https://www.house.gov/representatives/find-your-representative

She Should Run (https://www.sheshouldrun.org/) is a nonpartisan group that helps women get elected to office

Emerge America (https://emergeamerica.org/) prepares women who identify as Democrats to run for office.

National Federation of Republican Women - provides resources and tools for women who identify as Republicans. (http://www.nfrw.org/programs)

Higher Heights encourages and supports women of color to run for office. (http://www.higherheightsforamerica.org/)

More Women Leaders Needed Everywhere - a documentary by Kirthi Nath (https://cinemagicalmedia.com/portfolio-item/more-women-leaders-needed-everywhere/)

For Girls

One of our favorite sources of great information to help you raise empowered girls is *A Mighty Girl*. (www.amightygirl.com)

Global Girls Alliance (https://www.obama.org/globalgirlsalliance/)

Strong Girl Spirit (https://stronggirlspirit.com/)

Courageous Girl (http://www.courageousgirl.com/)

GREAT CHILDREN'S BOOKS ABOUT ACTIVISM AND DISSENT:

I Am Rosa Parks
Written by: Brad Meltzer
Illustrated by: Christopher Eliopoulos

I Dissent: Ruth Bader Ginsburg Makes Her Mark
Written by: Debbie Levy
Illustrated by: Elizabeth Baddeley

We Will Not Be Silent: The White Rose Student Resistance Movement that Defied Adolf Hitler
Written by: Russell Freedman

Separate Is Never Equal: Sylvia Mendez and Her Family's Fight for Desegregation
Written by: Duncan Tonatiuh
Illustrated by: Duncan Tonatiuh

Heart On Fire: Susan B. Anthony Votes for President
Written by: Ann Malaspina
Illustrated by: Steve James

Marching With Aunt Susan: Susan B. Anthony and the Fight for Women's Suffrage
Written by: Claire Rudolf Murphy
Illustrated by: Stacey Schuett

The Youngest Marcher: The Story of Audrey Faye Hendricks, a Young Civil Rights Activist
    Written by: Cynthia Levinson
    Illustrated by: Vanessa Brantley Newton

Elizabeth Warren: Nevertheless, She Persisted
Written by: Susan Wood
Illustrated by: Sarah Green

Let It Shine: Stories of Black Women Freedom Fighters
Written by: Andrea Davis Pinkney
Illustrated by: Stephen Alcorn

*Fannie Never Flinched: One Woman's Courage in the Struggle for American Labor Union Right*s
    Written by: Mary Cronk Farrell

www.ingramcontent.com/pod-product-compliance
Lightning Source LLC
Chambersburg PA
CBHW052133110526
44591CB00012B/1697